Demos is an independent think tank committed to radical thinking on the long-term problems facing the UK and other advanced industrial societies.

It aims to develop ideas – both theoretical and practical – to help shape the politics of the twenty first century, and to improve the breadth and quality of political debate.

Demos publishes books and a regular journal and undertakes substantial empirical and policy oriented research projects. Demos is a registered charity.

In all its work Demos brings together people from a wide range of backgrounds in business, academia, government, the voluntary sector and the media to share and cross-fertilise ideas and experiences.

For further information and
subscription details please contact:
Demos
Panton House
25 Haymarket
London SW1Y 4EN
Telephone: 0171 321 2200
Facsimile: 0171 321 2342
email: mail@demos.co.uk

The analysis and recommendations in this report do not necessarily reflect the policies of the organisations which supported the research.

THE CREATIVE AGE

Knowledge and skills for the new economy

Kimberly Seltzer and Tom Bentley

First published in 1999 by
Demos
Panton House
25 Haymarket
London SW1Y 4EN
Telephone: 0171 321 2200
Facsimile: 0171 321 2342

email: mail@demos.co.uk

ISBN 1 898309 898 309 70 1
Printed in Great Britain by Redwood Books, Trowbridge
Design by Lindsay Nash

Contents

Acknowledgements

We are grateful to the following people for their invaluable help in completing this project: Emma Garman, Ravi Gurumurthy, Tom Hampson, Ben Jupp, Gavin Mensah-Coker, Lindsay Nash, Charles and Elizabeth Handy, Sir Douglas Hague, Charles Leadbeater, Philip Adey, Jonathan Briggs, Ned Rimer, Cathie Jenkins, Courtney Welsh, Frank Nigriello, Ian Campbell, Julian Sefton-Green, Alison Huxley, Martin Brown, Shelagh Wright, Tim Oates, Andy Green, Alison Wolfe, Edwin Moses, Frank Levy, Linda Denello, Celia Greenwood, Maggie Farrar, Rebecka Lindberg, Mattais Nystrom, Karl Andersson, Palsule Sudhanshu and Dan Pronovost.

Executive summary

1.   For the first time in history, knowledge is the primary source of economic productivity. It has begun to penetrate most of the products that we create, and become a core resource for organisations and an emblem of individual employability. Technological progress, organisational change and intensified global competition have driven a shift from manual work to 'thinking' jobs that emphasise a whole new range of skills, from problem-solving and communication to information and risk management and self-organisation.

2.   Yet while the underlying economic structures of society are undergoing a dramatic transformation, our educational structures are lagging behind. The challenge of delivering an expanding set of skills and competencies is being partially met by the creation of a new lifelong learning infrastructure. However, innovations in lifelong learning continue to exist on the fringes of our education system. The dominant educational paradigm still focuses on *what* students know, rather than *how* they use that knowledge.

3.   In contrast to the typical worker of the industrial era who was required to learn a relatively stable set of competencies, the knowledge-based worker is experiencing a blurring of boundaries between work and learning. Those unable to update their knowledge base fast enough, both on the job and on their own time, are increasingly at risk of marginalisation, competing within a shrinking set of low-skill vocations.

4.   While qualifications are still integral to personal success, it is no longer enough for students to show that they are capable of passing public examinations. To thrive in an economy defined by the innovative application of knowledge, we must be able to do more than absorb and feedback information. Learners and workers must draw on their entire spectrum of learning experiences and apply what they have learned in new and

creative ways. A central challenge for the education system is therefore to find ways of embedding learning in a range of meaningful contexts, where students can use their knowledge and skills creatively to make an impact on the world around them.

5.   This report argues that creativity can be learned and presents leading examples from different sectors of society of how it can be done. It argues that to realise the creative potential of all citizens, and to boost competitiveness in the knowledge economy, we must make radical changes to the education system. In particular, we must restructure the school curriculum to reflect forms of learning which develop creative ability.

6.   In contrast to more traditional notions of what it means to 'be creative', we argue that creativity is not an individual characteristic or innate talent. Creativity is the application of knowledge and skills in new ways to achieve a valued goal. To achieve this, creative learners must have four key qualities:

- the ability to identify new problems, rather than depending on others to define them
- the ability to transfer knowledge gained in one context to another in order to solve a problem
- a belief in learning as an incremental process, in which repeated attempts will eventually lead to success
- the capacity to focus attention in the pursuit of a goal, or set of goals.

7.   Creativity, however, cannot be learned in a vacuum. Rather than a being a skill which can be performed on command, it is a form of interaction between the learner and her environment. Our case studies, and other evidence, reveal key characteristics of learning environments that encourage creativity.

- ***Trust:*** secure, trusting relationships are essential to environments in which people are prepared to take risks and are able to learn from failure.
- ***Freedom of action:*** creative application of knowledge is only possible where people are able to make real choices over what they do and how they try to do it.
- ***Variation of context:*** learners need experience applying their skills in a range of contexts in order to make connections between them.

- **The right balance between skills and challenge:** creativity emerges in environments where people are engaged in challenging activities and have the right level of skill to meet them.
- **Interactive exchange of knowledge and ideas:** creativity is fostered in environments where ideas, feedback and evaluation are constantly exchanged, and where learners can draw on diverse sources of information and expertise.
- **Real world outcomes:** creative ability and motivation are reinforced by the experience of making an impact – achieving concrete outcomes, changing the way that things are done.

8. This report is based on case studies of five innovative programmes which provide valuable lessons about cultivating and assessing creativity. Citizens Schools is an out-of-school learning programme for nine to fourteen year olds in Boston, Massachusetts, which uses over 1,000 volunteer professionals as apprentice–teachers in a range of fields. Harlem Educational Activities Fund, in New York City, is an enrichment programme for twelve to 21 year olds that wraps a spectrum of services around the needs of its students to help them gain acceptance to competitive secondary schools and colleges, and to thrive in these environments. Hyper Island, in Karlskrona, Sweden is a new kind of university which teaches its students the New Media Design trade through hands-on 'live projects' and work placements. Waterloo University's Co-operative Education programme, in Canada, has integrated the notion of work-based learning into the more traditional university environment, offering students opportunities to spend up to half of their college careers applying their skills and knowledge in professional settings. Unipart Group is a manufacturing firm in Oxford that has infused creative learning into the life of its employees through its in-house university and innovative creative problem solving process.

9. These case studies lead us to a series of conclusions about what a policy agenda for creativity should look like. Rather than trying to increase skills levels through conventional qualifications, government should take a different approach to educating for creativity. Alongside the new lifelong learning infrastructure, school education must be restructured to ensure that every individual has the skills and confidence to make full use of the opportunities that a knowledge-based society presents.

   Basic skills such as literacy, numeracy and core subject disciplines will continue to be important. However, if they are taught in ways that do not facilitate their transfer and application to a range of different contexts, their value will not be realised.

Creative application of knowledge cannot be learned and practised within a predefined curriculum structure if it is focused too heavily on content, at the expense of depth of understanding and breadth of application. Government should therefore put in place a range of policies to support the development of independent, creative and rigorous lifelong learners. Our main recommendations are:

- Reduce National Curriculum content requirements by half, in order to create space for a broader range of learning experience and achieving genuine understanding in each discipline.
- Develop a curriculum model that includes extended project-based learning in a range of contexts.
- Ensure that every school student has an IT-based Learning Portfolio – the spine of a new lifelong learning career.
- Appoint at least two school–community brokers to every school, to co-ordinate learning projects and placements, and create a network of information, support and learning opportunities
- Develop new skill specifications, based on the clusters of skills we set out in chapter three. These specifications would set out in detail the skills and abilities that should be embedded in every learning experience. They should not be seen as separate from other subjects and disciplines but be integrated into the study of all subjects.
- Create financial incentives and practical support to ensure that half of undergraduates undertake an extended work placement as part of their degree.
- Reward and disseminate creative input by policy makers, public servants, teachers and lecturers by adjusting professional contracts and creating 'innovation funds'.
- Create a series of databases, linked to the National Grid for Learning and the University for Industry, to match learners with placement opportunities, mentors and ideas that they can apply creatively.
- Develop new models of inter-disciplinary teaching and learning, and adjust teacher training courses to reflect them.

These changes would provoke controversy and resistance. But only radical action will ensure that the UK makes the most of the opportunities presented by the knowledge economy, and that every individual has the capacities and confidence to thrive in the new environment.

– 1 –

Creativity and the knowledge economy

Knowledge has become the primary resource of the new economy. As a result, the ways in which people acquire and use it have taken on a new significance. As Charles Leadbeater puts it, in the next century

> 'the engine of growth will be the process through which an economy creates, applies and extracts value from knowledge.'[1]

Driven by the increasing impact of information and communications technologies and by economic globalisation, the shift from an industrial to a knowledge-based economy means profound changes in the ways we work, live and learn. Four key trends are driving the demand for more, and different, skills.

- The 'weightless' economy:[2] intangible resources such as information, organisational networks and human capital have become the primary sources of productivity and competitiveness.
- Weightless work: the number of part-time, temporary, fixed contract and self employed workers has also risen steadily in the last half-century. Workers must increasingly manage themselves in a more fluid and unstable organisational environment.
- The networked economy: digital technology, organisational restructuring and higher volumes of information are generating a shift from vertical to horizontal relationships within and between organisations. Networks are becoming a basic organisational form.
- Knowledge and skill exclusion: the increasing premium on new skills and qualifications is creating new patterns of marginalisation among those who lack the means or motivation to acquire marketable knowledge. Developing new kinds of skills are central to their future prospects.

These changes have clear implications for individuals and organisations in the knowledge economy: all contribute to the need for greater creative ability.

- More and more work will require a high knowledge component and high level skills; even marginal and low-paying jobs will demand greater ability to manage information, apply knowledge and learn on the job.
- Accelerating competition and the application of new technologies mean that companies must innovate more rapidly in order to survive. This innovative pressure applies to new product and service development, to communication and to management and employment practice.
- Combined disciplines and knowledge bases, for example the combination of artistic and technical skills, or of professional knowledge and inter-personal ability, will be increasingly important to maximising the value of 'intellectual capital'.
- Increasingly, people will need to rely on themselves to manage, organise and balance their lives. The changing patterns and demands of the labour market will require new forms of personal discipline and self-reliance.

THE 'WEIGHTLESS' ECONOMY

A primary feature of the knowledge-driven economy is the growing importance of intangible resources: information, human capital, research and development, brands and organisational networks. A recent study by the Brookings Institution of more than 2,000 US firms found that physical assets accounted for less than a third of their market value. Between 1970 and 1990, industrial employment, based mainly on material resources and assets, declined by 15 per cent in the UK, 12 per cent in Netherlands and 10 per cent in Australia, Germany and Sweden and more marginal declines in Japan and the US.[3] During this same twenty-year period, employment in the service sector, which incorporates most knowledge work, has expanded in the US, Canada, Australia, Japan, France, Germany, Italy, Netherlands, Sweden and the UK. In 1970 'weightless' service sector work accounted for between 40 and 63 per cent of total employment. By 1990 the service sector accounted for 60 per cent to 70 per cent of total civilian employment across the US, Canada, Australia, Japan, France Germany Italy Netherlands Sweden and the United Kingdom.[4] The EU's five largest growth sectors – business services, health care, education, recreational activities, and hotels and restaurants – produced more than 70 per cent of employment growth between 1994 and 1997.[5]

'Intellectual property' sectors are now growing at twice the rate of the US economy and generating work at three times the rate. In the UK, the creative industries[6] have grown by 34 per cent in the past decade.[7] The Department of Culture, Media and Sport has estimated that these industries generate more than £57 billion per year in revenues and currently employ more than 1.7 million people, over 5 per cent of the total employed workforce.[8]

WEIGHTLESS WORK

In occupational terms, the demand for labour has become more heavily skewed towards the knowledge intensive professional and technical occupations. For example, Between 1979 and 1996, the percentage of high-skill jobs in the US rose from 34 to roughly 40 per cent.[9] In the EU as a whole, this trend has been characterised by a growth of approximately 1 per cent a year in management and professional technical jobs, 0.2 per cent per year for sales and service jobs and losses of 0.5 per cent a year in agriculture, craft, and elementary jobs.[10] In the UK, the percentage of total employment accounted for by managerial/professional/technical workers rose from 29 per cent to 36.5 per cent between 1984 and 1997, while the proportion of manual workers fell from 40.6 per cent to 29.7 per cent.[11] By 2005, it is predicted that professional and technical workers will account for 4 per cent more employment than any other sector in the US, with professional and technical occupations accounting for one in four new jobs created between 1991 and 2005.[12]

Alongside the shift towards 'pure' knowledge jobs, other forms of employment increasingly require the use and application of knowledge. Involvement in process reengineering, quality programmes and cross-functional teams are now part of routine job requirements. Even in manufacturing, standardised work routines are being replaced by more complex processes involving the application of higher order thinking skills that were once associated only with white collar work. Computer technologies do not simply automate, but more importantly they 'informate',[13] allowing production operators to access previously inaccessible information, and creating demand for problem-solving and analytical skills. At the same time, companies increasingly rely on temporary and outsourced labour. In 1999, one in three college graduates in Britain entered fixed-term or temporary jobs, evidence of a growing trend towards contingent employment.[14] By 1993, 65 per cent of America's fast-track firms were contracting out for labour-intensive services that were once carried out in-house.[15] Self-employment is also rising steadily in both the UK and the US.

For some, 'weightlessness' presents new opportunities to apply what they know in multiple work contexts, diversifying their range of skills and knowledge through a portfolio career structure.[16] For others, the consequences include low pay, poor benefits, and insecurity.

These changes mean that workers need a new range of skills, not just to fulfill their job requirements, but to organise and manage their own lives effectively.

THE NETWORKED ECONOMY

The new economy also gives a central role to networks – virtual, organisational and social. Digital technology is creating an economy based on immediacy and virtualisation, and generating new organisational structures and relationships. Information, education, training, products and services are expected to be delivered on demand, at the time and place they are wanted. Networks have emerged as the organisational form most suited to meeting these demands, in contrast to more rigid, hierarchical structures.

For companies, networks can provide unlimited access to the most innovative products and processes and ensure competitive advantage at home and abroad. Equally important, networks are self-reinforcing – organisations become increasingly attractive to potential partners as their connections multiply.

The growing importance of specialist workers and increasing pressure for innovation have also increased the need for horizontal networks within organisations. As niche markets expand and work becomes more technical and domain-specific, the need for collaboration between workers increases massively. Centralised control and management structures can no longer handle information flows within and between organisations, while at the same time allowing autonomous decision-making and collaboration at the frontline. Because managers have increasingly less specialised knowledge than the workers they supervise, horizontal teams and networks become more productive methods of organising tasks.[17] This process of organisational flattening has resulted in smaller, more customer-oriented units or project teams made up of employees with diverse skills and specialisms.

KNOWLEDGE AND SKILLS EXCLUSION

While skills levels overall rose in Britain between 1986 and 1997, workers in more marginal forms of employment are significantly less likely to receive training in areas that will enhance their employability. A man on a temporary or fixed term contract is 19 per cent less likely to receive training in his current job than a man on permanent contract, while a comparable women is 14 per cent less likely. Part-time male workers are 8 per cent less likely to receive work-related training than full-time men, and women in part-time work are 10 per cent less likely to undergo work-related training.[18] Other groups vulnerable to skills exclusion include the self-employed, workers over 50, non-college graduates and low-paid workers.[19] American economists have estimated that young people entering the labour market without university qualifications hold on average six different jobs and experience four to five periods of unemployment between eighteen and 27, and earn dramatically less than their degree holding counterparts.[20]

Industries reporting the highest levels of skills gaps are the least likely to provide employee training. In 1998, the British manufacturing, hotels and catering and retail industries had the lowest proportion of employers providing training to their workforce (31 per cent, 41 per cent and 41 per cent respectively), while reporting the highest gaps in skills (15 per cent, 17 per cent and 13 per cent). Conversely the industries with the best track record of employee training- financial services, the public sector and the personal and protective services (79 per cent, 76 per cent and 60 per cent respectively) had significantly lower percentages of workers with skill gaps – 2 per cent in the financial services, 11 per cent in the public sector and 2 per cent in the personal and protective services.

These new divisions help clarify the skills challenge. If work and wealth are increasingly based on the application of know-how, then the potential to contribute and share in them is greatly increased. Many more jobs will involve creative input, analysis and variation, as opposed to hard physical labour and mind-numbing routine. However, variations in social class, family support, income and access to learning opportunities create new patterns of inequality and division. Starting from a marginal position in the knowledge society greatly increases the risk of later disadvantage. Being unable to grasp opportunities at each stage of life or work can make it harder and harder to adapt. But governments are less able to compensate for these problems simply by providing security: instead they must support people to adapt and to transfer skills and knowledge from one context to another.

Using knowledge creatively is central to realising economic and social value, and to developing individual potential to thrive. It is as important to overcoming exclusion as it is to competitiveness in the high-value, high-reward sectors of the economy. In many ways, the rising importance of creativity is driven by the emergence of a knowledge-based economy. However, creativity is also vital to meeting the social, political and cultural challenges of the next century. Institutional renewal, community regeneration, and the capacity of politics to solve emerging problems all depend on our ability to marshal the full range of knowledge resources, and to use them in the most effective ways.

– 2 –

The skills challenge

In 1998, over two-thirds of British employers believed that the skills needed in their average employee were increasing. The most common explanations included changes in processes and technology, increased emphasis on multi-skilling and greater focus on customer care.[21] While expectations rise, the evidence suggests a dearth of suitably skilled people.[22] Overall, skills shortages in Britain have reached the highest level since before the last recession,[23] and economists predict that the number of hard-to-fill-vacancies will continue to rise. In the US the number of companies suffering skill shortages has doubled, with almost seven out of ten reporting a lack of skilled entry-level workers.[24] In many sectors, it seems impossible that conventional approaches to training and education will be able to meet the escalating demand for new skills.

INVESTING IN KNOWLEDGE

Just as government spending on education is rising, more companies are also offering employees support to develop their careers on their own time.[25] United Technologies, for example, offers employees a range of incentives for pursuing coursework, including paying their tuition fees (up to $70,000 for MBA coursework) and granting 100 shares of company stock to all those who complete a degree.[26] In the UK, the reported application of high level skills has risen from 16.2 per cent in 1986 to 18.4 per cent in 1997 and the proportion of jobs with long-term training requirements (two years or more) has jumped by more than a quarter in the past eleven years, from 22 per cent to 28 per cent.[27] Employee education is growing 100 times (10,000 per cent) faster than academia.[28] This growth in privately financed, employee-focused learning will continue to escalate, making up more and more of the educational infrastructure. But even this sea-change is not enough to ensure that skill needs are met, let alone that every individual gets the chance to realise her full potential. The kinds of knowledge and skills required by the new economy are different in many ways from the core knowledge needed for security and prosperity over the past hundred years.

CHANGING DEMANDS

As conditions change more rapidly, companies are more likely to recruit for adaptability and fresh ideas rather than standardised skills and experience. This is reflected in the shift away from industry specific skills and competencies towards more personal qualities and 'soft' skills such as communication, teamwork, reliability, problem solving, positive attitudes towards learning and the capacity to manage one's own training.[29] Too much experience is increasingly viewed as a competitive disadvantage, as the more experienced workers command more pay, while requiring substantial training.[30]

As explained by a long-time employee and human resources director at Ford Motor Company, in the 1960s, hiring an employee was merely a 'warm body process': 'If we had a vacancy, we would look outside in the plant waiting room to see if there are any warm bodies standing there. If someone was there and they looked physically ok and they weren't an obvious alcoholic, they were hired.'[31]

Now companies like Ford, Chrysler and Honda go to great lengths to find employees who not only demonstrate secondary school level numeracy and literacy skills, but also the capacity for higher order thinking, effective communication and team working. At Diamond-Chrysler Motors, for example, job applicants fill out forms which include questions about educational attainment and employment history. They then take an examination called the General Aptitude Test Battery that tests for nine different 'hard' skills, including numerical and verbal aptitude. If they make the cutoff and pass the physical exam and drug tests, they are then tested for mechanical aptitude using another standardised test called the Bennet Mechanical Comprehension Test. Finally, they participate in hands-on assessments which measure less tangible skills such as oral communication, inter-personal skills and problem-solving skills. One test, for example, involves working with a team of people to fashion a product without the benefit of any blueprint or guide as to how the product should be constructed. The only thing that applicants have available to them are a set of raw materials and a picture of what the final product should look like.[32]

This example illustrates a fundamental change in the skills needed for work. Over the past three generations, people have been able to build up their knowledge and skills through a linear process, leading from basic education into more specalised training and then into work. Not only have the levels of knowledge required for work risen, but the *kinds* of knowledge required have also changed.

THE SKILLS PARADOX

This leads to a paradox. While skills requirements are rising, more qualifications are not necessarily helpful. Because of the premium on new ideas and flexibility, people who have built up detailed knowledge over time find them-selves at a disadvantage if they do not know how to apply what they know in different ways. The 'new basic skills'[33] are about *how* people think and act, not just what they know.

In the meantime, qualifications are still at premium because they act as a form of currency and a mark of status. Most employers still use them as a way of sorting job applicants, even if they claim that they are looking for other kinds of ability. We are increasingly looking to schools and universities to deliver different *kinds* of knowledge and skills, while also augmenting the pres-sure for them to deliver conventional qualifications.

As a result, education systems are trying to deliver a wider range of out-comes perhaps than ever before. Emotional, parenting and relationship skills, citizenship and civic virtues, business and enterprise skills, problem-solving and analytical skills, motivational and leadership skills are all called for, while the pressure to learn more traditional subjects remains as strong as ever.

This paradox leads us to two main conclusions. The first is that, to meet esca-lating demands, the education system itself needs a greater capacity for inno-vation and creativity. Making more effective use of resources, creating and applying knowledge in new ways, are as important to education as to any other sector. Second, we must recognise that innovation partly depends on being able to leave behind established assumptions and educational methods which may have outlived their usefulness. The education system will be unable to innovate effectively unless it can create a new space in which to do it. Simply adding to the list of requirements and outcomes, even with increased spend-ing, is not enough if we are looking for education to deliver different *kinds* of outcome.

FUTURE SKILLS

The central theme underpinning this new demand for skills is creativity: the ability to apply and generate knowledge in a range of contexts, in order to meet a specific goal in a new way. Before we turn to what creativity is, and how it can be learned, we also need to be clearer about what kinds of skills will be more important in the new economy. We do not attempt a definitive list. Instead, we set out clusters of skills and knowledge that are emerging as pre-requisites for independence, self reliance and success.

Information management

The volume of information that we handle in daily life has grown exponential-ly with the advent of information and communications technologies. From the media to consumer product choices, executive decisions to production-line adjustments, we now have to cope with a welter of available information and be able to distinguish what is relevant and useful from the background noise.

To be effective, individuals must be able to select and organise information, as well as to absorb it. 'The problem isn't just in using information but being your own "editor-in-chief"', argues Francois Mariet, of the University of Paris-Dauphine. Knowing what information to look for is also integral to effective knowledge management. At BP Amoco, employees are appointed as 'knowledge guardians' whose job it is to explore the unknown and share their discoveries with project teams.[34] The central shift is from a model of learning and consumption which rested on established channels of information – textbooks, teachers, company research departments, newspapers – to one where there is a far larger and more chaotic range of data, accessed through more varied and fluid channels. Having access to the same information as everybody else is less and less valuable – finding new sources, and then synthesising them with the existing picture, is more and more important.

Self-organisation

People work and live in increasingly fluid environments. In most sectors, hierarchies and divisions of labour are becoming less rigid. From flexible hours to project-based work, self-employment to variation in family structure, organisational contexts are less fixed and predictable. One of the great changes in working life, lamented by sociologist Richard Sennett, is the loss of regular routine. This change gives a new onus to the skills of self-organisation – defining and structuring our objectives, managing our time, clarifying priorities, avoiding overwork, saving money, and juggling various and conflicting responsibilities. While school timetables still largely fix our objectives in advance and then teach us how to turn up on time and meet the demands of centralised schedule, contemporary work and lifestyles increasingly demand that we organise ourselves. Mental self-organisation is also growing in importance – developing thinking strategies, applying ourselves in different ways to a problem, and understanding the range of tools and techniques we can use to perform a task are all key to maximising our effectiveness.

Inter-disciplinary

The most valuable forms of innovation increasingly rely on the interface between different kinds of knowledge, for example the combination of new information technology with a new accounting system, or of design and technical skills in creating new websites. Management and business skills are more important, even for those who are not specialising in them, because of the growth of self-employment and the decentralisation of large organisations.

Technical and specialist knowledge have also become more valuable. Achieving depth of knowledge and understanding is therefore still crucial. But it is striking how often value is realised when different bodies of knowledge are brought together. This means that inter-disciplinary skills are more and more valuable to individuals and to organisations. Inter-disciplinary knowledge means far more than just specialisation in more than one subject. It requires the ability to understand the *interface* between different areas of knowledge, and to apply insights from one to the other. The vocabulary, technology, underlying structure and specific techniques of each discipline are often very different. Learning to translate from one to another, and to combine them in pursuit of a goal, takes particular kinds of practice and learning experience.

Personal and inter-personal

If work is increasingly integrated horizontally across teams and clusters, being able to interact successfully with other people is also more and more important. The growth of service industries, and the growing importance of client and customer service have also fuelled this change. Again the imperative is broader than just the economy – family relationships, subject to unprecedented pressures and sustained less and less by the structures and assumptions of the past, also call for greater personal skills and self-awareness. Communities, as they become more diverse and in some cases less close-knit, also depend on their ability to communicate and co-operate over shared concerns and goals. Self-understanding, motivation, emotional awareness and inter-personal skill have all become more familiar in the educational debate, but they have not yet achieved the central place in educational practice that they will have to assume.

Tied to these relationship skills is communication – at the interface between inter-personal and information skills – the ability to convey information in effective and appropriate ways. Individuals will need to be able to articulate their knowledge, experiences and feelings in order to work effectively in teams, market their talent, forge alliances and seek out new information.

While most people tend to view communication as a straightforward process of verbalisation and listening, psychologists such as Howard Gardner and David Perkins have suggested that there are multiple avenues for communication.[35] Multi-medium communication, or the ability to rely on a range of techniques for articulating one's thoughts and experiences, forms the foundation for effective interaction. There are a number of avenues through which one can build bridges between communicator and receiver. Some involve verbal techniques such as analogies, metaphors and stories, some on visual techniques such as diagrams, outlines and photographs, others rely on audio techniques such as music, and of course the use of multimedia to communicate has become an ever more popular means of communicating information. Bipin Junnarkar, President and Chief Executive Officer of Datafusion Inc, an information technology consulting service, encourages his employees to use storytelling and photography as a means of sharing information. Instead of asking his employees to take notes at business conferences and present them formally to their co-workers afterwards, they take pictures and use them to generate a story about their experience. The listeners write down the most interesting aspects of these experiences on index cards and these are collected and combined to form a trip report. Like many of his contemporaries, Junnarkar finds that his employees are much more interested in taking photos than taking notes, and that the employees on the receiving end of the communication process are also more engaged and reflective.[36]

Reflection and evaluation

As organisations come to see themselves as 'learning' and 'thinking' environments they are discovering that reflective capacity – the ability to draw upon, analyse and form decisions about themselves – is a vital part of their ability to adapt, respond and thrive. One implication of the shift to a knowledge-based society is that intelligence is far more evenly *distributed* than in previous eras. Where reflection has often been the preserve of relatively few institutions: the church, universities, some sections of the media, reflective capacity is now spreading far more widely across society as education levels rise and more organisations develop an ability to think and evaluate for themselves.

Reflection is integral to value. We can only learn to value something properly if we can distance ourselves from it, consider its importance in the wider scheme of things, and analyse its importance to other parts of our experience. Similarly, an organisation cannot identify the reasons why it has succeeded, or failed, in a particular area without being able to reflect on the different elements of what it has been doing. This is partly why reflective, or meta-cognitive skills, are becoming such an important feature of successful educational development.

Reflection is also instrumental to learning how we as individuals can form and develop our *goals*. This, as we will see in the next chapter, is a crucial element of creativity which has often been neglected by education. Increasing our personal effectiveness, creativity and ability to adapt is impossible without the capacity to form our own goals in life.

Risk

The final cluster of skills are those connected to managing risk. The risks that we face – of poor health, unemployment, dislocation, and so on – have changed massively over the past 40 years. Risk has in many ways become more individualised – employers and governments have retreated from protecting people against certain kinds of risk. More detailed information and greater consumer choice has led to the individualisation, for example of insurance products. When external conditions are less certain, when there are more choices to be made and a greater range of possible outcomes, people need to be able to understand, evaluate and live with risk, rather than simply trying to eliminate or ignore it. This is true in making life decisions – such as whether to invest in a particular fund, to start a new business, to move cities in search of work, or to take time off for learning or parenting. It is also true at work, where employees are called on more often to absorb business risks – through contracting out and downsizing, for example – and to contribute to strategic decisions.

Living with risk is difficult and stressful, and becomes more complex as the risks that we face are increasingly 'manufactured' by science and human action. But risk management is essential to thriving in the new economy. It calls for a set of skills to be far more widely distributed across the population:

- *futures thinking:* being able to imagine and analyse different future scenarios and their implications
- *decision-making:* being able to think through the available options, and make clear decisions about the best one
- *stress management:* knowing how to cope with tension and direct one's energy in healthy ways
- *learning from failure:* being able to translate one's mistakes or shortcomings into opportunities for learning.

These clusters of skills and knowledge will become increasingly important to success and well-being. But we must not fall into the trap of thinking that they can simply be added to the formal curriculum. There are too many skills and competing kinds of knowledge for them all to be squeezed into the limited time and space allowed by our current educational frameworks. And the central lesson of successful innovation is that such skills can only be useful when they are applied in the right ways, according to the purpose in mind, and the specific context. Whatever knowledge and skills we might have, the central challenge is to find ways of applying them *creatively*. In the next chapter we turn to what this means.

– 3 –

Understanding creativity

Listing the skills that are becoming more important is one step towards helping people to thrive in a knowledge economy, but it is not enough. We must also identify the most effective ways to teach and learn them, and make sure that our educational frameworks reflect this. This causes a problem, because of the ever-growing list of outcomes which education is expected to produce, and the inflexibility of the framework within which it operates.

One response to this challenge is to say that people need a set of general skills or competencies which are common to everything, and which go alongside whatever specific knowledge they are learning. A clear illustration of this in the UK is the specification of six 'Key Skills' – communication, application of number, working with others, use of information technology, problem solving and improving one's own learning and performance – which all students are expected to develop.

But schools and colleges have found it difficult to know how to incorporate these skills into their teaching and assessment strategies. In particular 'softer' skills, such as improving one's own learning and performance, run against the grain of the National Curriculum assessment regime and of separate subject-based teaching. The problems experienced with Key Skills help to illustrate the need for a different approach.

It is difficult to develop separate qualifications for them when they are mainly learned through their *application* to a wide range of contexts. The problem of trying to cram an ever-growing set of skills into limited space and time is not solved by a general framework, unless we can find practical ways to learn and teach them across the whole of the curriculum. Current divisions between courses, subjects, and assessment schemes make this a daunting task.

We believe the key challenge is to shift the focus away from what people should *know* and onto what they should be able *to do* with their knowledge. This is central to developing creative ability.

But what does it really mean to be creative? Creativity is one of the most contested and misunderstood concepts in the vocabulary. The term brings to mind many different qualities and ideas, often in tension with each other. This chapter sets out some essential elements of creative ability, and the conditions needed to foster it.

WHAT CREATIVITY IS NOT

- The most common misconception about creativity is that it involves artistic sensibility. But despite the growing importance of creative and cultural industries, creativity has always extended much further. Albert Einstein, Steven Hawking and Madame Curie were no less creative in their contributions to their fields than Picasso or Shakespeare.
- Secondly, creativity is not equivalent to brilliance. While some people may be fascinating to talk to, or may express novel thoughts, they are not necessarily more creative than others.
- Thirdly, creativity does not automatically imply talent. Someone may have an innate ability to do something well, or to model their work after respected people in their field – yet there is no guarantee that she will use her talent to make her own creative contributions.
- Finally and most importantly, creativity is not a skill. It is not simply a technique that one can perform well on command.

UNDERSTANDING CREATIVITY

This report argues that creativity has as much to do with what people *do not know* as with what they do. It requires the ability to solve problems progressively over time and apply previous knowledge to new situations. Creativity is also bound up with context – it can only be defined and assessed in relation to the context in which it is achieved. It must be developed through the interaction of the learner, her underlying goals and motivations, and the resources and context in which she operates. Four main characteristics define the creative, or progressive problem-solver.

- The ability to formulate new problems, rather than depending on others to define them.
- The ability to transfer what one learns across different contexts.
- The ability to recognise that learning is incremental and involves making mistakes.
- The capacity to focus one's attention in pursuit of a goal.

Finding problems

'Thinking,' in the words of psychologist David Perkins, 'is what we do when we do not know'.[37] Along these lines, a creative learner needs to be of the mindset that success does not just come from being an expert, but also from the process of learning in areas that are unfamiliar, thus expanding the limits of their expertise and inventing new areas for others to explore. This creative process, of constantly pushing the boundaries of an activity or field, has been referred to as 'progressive problem-solving',[38] or 'learning your way around'.[39] The progressive problem-solver recognises that activities present ongoing challenges, and welcomes these challenges as opportunities to build knowledge. More importantly, the progressive problem-solver is not only capable of solving 'presented problems'[40] that have been formulated by others – he discovers new problems when others may not even be asking any questions at all. As physicist Freeman Dyson puts it, 'it is characteristic of scientific life that it is easy when you have a problem to work on. The hard part is finding your problem.'[41]

So the most creative learners are not necessarily those who are most adept or who know all the answers, but those who can formulate the kinds of questions that lead them on a constant path of learning, discovery and invention. They are people who have learned how to apply knowledge and skills across contexts in order to solve problems, but more importantly they also know how to use their reserve of knowledge and skills to identify new problems.

Transferring knowledge across contexts

How does one learn to be a good 'problem-finder'? In other words how does one learn to apply their knowledge and skills when there is no impetus from outside, or problem put before them by another? Here the concept of 'transfer' is very helpful. Psychologists have distinguished between two kinds of transfer, near transfer and far transfer. Near transfer simply means that one has applied what he or she knows in highly similar contexts, as in the case of someone who transfers her knowledge of how to drive a car into the context of driving a truck. Far transfer involves a bigger conceptual hurdle, as in the case of someone transferring her knowledge of geometry to the game of billiards. Perkins and his colleague Gavriel Salomon distinguish between two mechanisms of transfer, the 'low road' and the 'high road'. Low road transfer occurs when the perceptual similarities of one problem to another automatically trigger a connection. This process transpires more often for those who have had ample opportunity to practice using a particular skill or knowledge in comparable situations. High road transfer, on the other hand, involves active reflection on the connections between problems and requires the application of skills and knowledge in diverse situations.

The lesson here is that creative learners need a wider array of contexts within which to apply their skills and knowledge. They also need 'teachers', or guides who can expose them to strategies for thinking about the connections between their experiences. The more explicit the reflection process is and the wider diversity of problem contexts, the more likely it is that a person will learn how to make connections on their own.

Recognising that learning is incremental

Some learners are more likely than others to not only use their available knowledge and skills, but more importantly, to persist with their learning when things seem beyond their grasp. For example, psychologist Carol Dweck has distinguished between two types of dispositions to learning. 'Entity learners', on the one hand, believe that when learning you either understand something right away or you don't. In contrast, 'incremental learners' see learning as a gradual process requiring repeated effort, and often mistakes. While the entity learner may be technically skilled, she is more disposed to giving up if understanding does not come quickly. The incremental learner, on the other hand, is at an advantage (regardless of skill level) when tackling unfamiliar or challenging situations, as her belief in progressive learning fuels her willingness to invest herself in finding creative ways around a problem.[42]

Often advocates of skills equate the possession of skills with a guarantee that people automatically recognise and take advantage of opportunities to use them. But this assumption neglects the fact that the application and development of skills and knowledge vary significantly according to one's individual disposition, or outlook. As explained by Perkins, 'dispositions shape our lives. They are proclivities that lead us in one direction rather than another within the freedom of action that we have.'[43] No matter how adept a person may be in a given area or set of areas, if they are not disposed to investing their energy in using these skills when an occasion arises, the creative process is repressed.

Focusing attention

> 'We learn what is supposed to be worth seeing, what is not; what to
> remember and what to forget ...The only way to take control over the
> ownership of life is by learning to direct psychic energy (our attention)
> in line with our own intentions.'[44]

The term 'readiness' is widely used among educators and psychologists, reflecting the paramount role that ability and willingness to focus one's attention plays in intellectual and vocational development. Clearly some people are more ready to engage in any activity, or become involved with it in a focused manner.[45] They are usually the ones who carry within them a set of longer-term goals towards which they aspire, strategies to use in pursuit of these goals, skills and resources to implement these strategies and the expectation that they will be rewarded.[46] These individuals are not only motivated enough to engage in progressive learning, but they have learned how to focus their energy and attention in such a way that few opportunities for growth go unnoticed.

There is strong evidence that the ability to adapt and take advantage of change is inextricably linked with the ability to focus one's attention positively in the pursuit of goals.[47] For example, in one study of people who became severely handicapped by disease or accidents, a number of individuals were identified who had not only adapted well to their tragedy, but who felt that their lives had improved as a result of their loss. The distinguishing factor between these people and those who did not adapt so well to their circumstances was the fact that they chose to discipline their attention in such a way they were able to 'master their limitation'.[48] They learned how to find enjoyment from some of the most basic activities, such as walking, dressing or driving a car. One even became a swimming instructor, another an archery champion who beat his opponents while confined to a wheelchair.

So what does this all mean? First of all, it means that creative people view learning as an ongoing, incremental process. They are *adaptable* in that they don't see skills or knowledge as something you either have or you don't – they view them as learning 'realms'[49] with more limitless and contiguous boundaries. Secondly, it means that creative individuals can engage in progressive learning, the ability to uncover new problems and redefine old ones. They *anticipate* the problems that will lead to tomorrow's solutions and find novel ways to apply what they have learned in the past. Thirdly, it means that they have goals which drive their ongoing learning, and the discipline to focus their attention and energy in positive and original ways. They are *committed* to doing what it takes, however long it takes, to solve the problems that will help them to reach their goals.

THE CREATIVE SYSTEM

But not everything hinges on the individual: creativity cannot occur within a vacuum. People need a place, or a domain within which to carry out tasks – a set of boundaries against which they can push. 'Creativity,' Mihalyi Csiksentmihalyi explains, 'is any act, idea or product that changes an existing domain, or that transforms a domain into a new one.'[50] Domains, or 'realms', as Perkins calls them, are the arenas within which problems are solved.[51] They provide a context for the creative process, a set of rules and symbols that serve as a foundation for the process of problem solving. Science, for example, is a domain. At a smaller level, learning one's way around a particular location, such as an office or a college campus, means that one is operating within a domain. Sometimes new domains are formed as the result of the creative process, as in the case of new academic disciplines or sports. The Internet, hardly understood by most people only ten years ago, is now a domain affecting millions of people.

The idea of domains or realms gives us a way of framing the actions of a learner, and relating innovation to its context. It is powerful because it can be applied to any situation – whether in a highly specialised area of science or technology, or a familiar and common context like household budgeting. It reminds us that actions can only be creative in relation to their impact on the real world. But simply doing something differently is not enough to create value on its own: to be useful creativity must meet a purpose, and to do this its value must be judged or assessed.

This is where the idea of a field comes in: a field is the group of people who are recognised as authorities in a particular domain – whether academics evaluating subject knowledge, judges assessing sporting prowess or technology experts testing out new software programmes. These are the people who validate creativity, by recognising that a new way of doing something is valuable, an improvement on the past, a better way of achieving a goal or meeting a need.

Creativity, then can be understood through the interaction of the three points of the triangle (see Figure 1 opposite). For creativity to be recognised and sustained, it has to be recognised and validated by the field of those qualified to judge. This field will vary enormously according to the domain. In consumer markets, for example, the field is the paying customer, who will determine whether a product succeeds or fails. In specialised areas of academic knowledge the field will be largely made up of university professors. In managing social relationships, the field is the peer group. Whoever it is, the field is essential to determining the value of a creative action.

THE CREATIVE ENVIRONMENT

The challenge of learning creativity is therefore partly a question of environment. We cannot achieve it by looking purely at personal characteristics or knowledge. It is essential to create environments that cultivate the belief in progressive learning and the ability to remain focused in the face of uncertainty. There is no question that context plays a significant role in determining whether one makes use of existing skills and knowledge and seeks out creative ways to build on what they already know.[52] Even those who are usually able to transfer their skills and their readiness to engage across a wide range of contexts, are less likely to do so in certain environments. As pointed out by Perkins, 'transfer is not a free lunch.'[53]

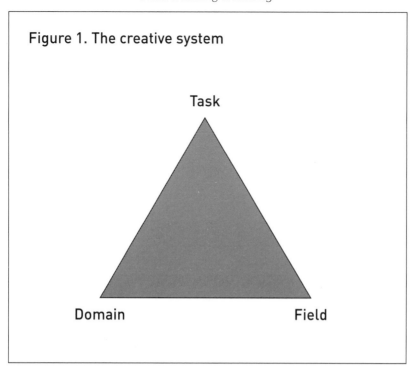

Figure 1. The creative system

Task

Domain   Field

In fact, critiques of the current approach to key skills assessment have centred around the lack of attention to the role of occupational and institutional environment in influencing whether skills are applied in different contexts.[54] Creativity is not a gene that is passed on, or an attribute that one possesses indefinitely. And nobody is a creative learner all the time. Creativity is an interaction between a learner and their environment.

This begs the question, what kinds of environments are more likely to foster creativity? Below is an initial list drawn from our case studies and other evidence.

Trust and support

The first thing we do when we enter a new environment is search for signals that we can trust those around us and that they will reciprocate this trust. This initial stage of involvement is passive, as we hold ourselves back from taking too many risks and observe our surroundings from a distance. Resolving this conflict between trust and mistrust is a fundamental determinant of the creative process. 'Am I safe here?', 'Do I belong?', 'Can I count on others to support me?', 'Should I stay?' The challenge, according to Dr Ronald Ferguson of Harvard University, is for organisations to communicate a sense of comfort and positive expectancy, so that individuals are ready to engage in the learning process. Impressions of the environment will continually change with each new experience. However, an ethos of trust inspires commitment to one's surroundings and allows creativity to take root.[55]

The programmes we have studied all succeed in building a foundation of trust and support that draws out the creative potential of individuals. At Citizen Schools and Hyper Island, for example, students participate in a spectrum of team-building and group processing activities, which generate a sense of community and inclusion. At Harlem Educational Activities Fund (HEAF) students see early on that the staff go above and beyond the call of duty to help them achieve their goals. It is not unusual for the programme's chief executive to get on a train and travel out of state when one of her college students is in need.

Freedom of action

According to psychologist Erik Erikson, once children learn to trust in their environment, they develop a 'sudden violent wish to have a choice.'[56] This need for freedom of action and self-control will continue to shape their self-esteem and sense of pride throughout their lives. 'From a sense of self-control' says Erikson 'without loss of self-esteem comes a lasting sense of good will and pride; from a sense of loss of self-control comes a lasting propensity for doubt and shame.'[57]

Even the most creative learners will be inhibited within a judgemental and constrictive environment. Conversely, the opportunity to act freely at work and in school reinforces the tendency to experiment and solve problems creatively. While the new economy rewards those who can adapt creatively to fluid and flexible markets, some argue that there have been no measurable increases in autonomy. 'Change', say Mulgan and Wilkinson 'is coming more by imposition and fear then as part of a rising tide of freedom.'[58]

Forward-thinking employers and educators, such as those described here, recognise that creativity cannot be imposed from without. Students and workers need more opportunities to discover and solve problems for themselves, without undue restrictions on the way they organise their time, their priorities and their personal responsibilities.

Unipart, for example, relies on its staff to manage their own time. At any given time of day, the exercise room, the technology centre, the health centre and the library will be filled with employees who choose to balance their work related activities with more personal ones. At Waterloo, students spend from sixteen to 24 months of their college careers developing their skills and knowledge while working in professional environments where they are given the freedom to manage their own work projects. Citizen Schools allows students to make their own choices about what careers they are interested in learning and encourages them to experiment without fear of making mistakes. And HEAF and Hyper Island take responsibilities such as grading, curriculum design, programme evaluation and planning and place them hands of the students.

Variation of context

Variation of context is crucial to creativity because it provides learners with opportunities to access different fields and to form new networks. There is no guarantee that individuals will apply 'old' skills and knowledge in new contexts. Moreover, those who do apply what they have learned may not do so in creative ways. However, when individuals have opportunities to transfer skills and knowledge across contexts, the creative process is set in motion.

As we saw above, two types of transfer can be cultivated within a creative environment, 'low road' and 'high road' transfer. The most creative environments provide opportunities for both. Environments that encourage low road transfer provide individuals with abundant practice at applying their skills and knowledge in different contexts with similar features. At Waterloo University and Hyper Island, for example, students practice skills in areas such as planning, collaboration and problem-solving in anywhere from three to six different work environments. Some students tend to seek out work placements that are similar in nature. But many, as we will see, take advantage of the opportunity to apply what they know in highly diverse sets of circumstances. Students may travel to different countries or explore an occupation that deviates from their individual course of study. When the same skill or knowledge is practiced over a wide variety of circumstances, it eventually results in the ability to make greater, more creative ' leaps' in skill and understanding.

'High Road' transfer involves actively searching for opportunities to apply what one knows in order to solve a problem. This approach involves active reflection on possible connections between domains. At HEAF, for example, chess students are challenged to make connections between the principles and strategies used in chess and those that apply to academic domains such as geography and physical science. A chess board becomes a medium for understanding concepts such as mass or latititude and longitude.

A balance between challenge and skills

Creativity, points out Csiksentmihalyi, depends on a proper balance between a person's skill level and the degree to which their are challenged by a task. When a person's skills are outweighed by the high level of challenge required by an activity, the result is often a state of anxiety. Conversely, activities which are not challenging enough to match the level of skills that one possesses tend to produce a feeling of boredom. When an activity is not challenging enough and when a person's skills are underutilised, one is likely to have an exceptionally low quality experience, characterised by apathy and indifference. Ideally, says, Csiksentmihalyi, activities require both a high level of skill as well as high level of challenge:

> 'When a person's skill is just right to cope with the demands of a situation – and when compared to the entirety of everyday life the demands are above average – the quality of experience improves noticeably....
> Even a frustrating job may suddenly become exciting if one hits upon the right balance.'[59]

At Unipart, employees are encouraged to constantly push themselves to find more effective and productive ways of working. Yet they are not expected to do so without assistance in developing their skills. All staff have the opportunity to take advantage of the course at Unipart's in-house university and they are allowed to do so as a part of their daily work routine. At Hyper Island, students are expected to take on roles and manage projects that are beyond their specialisation. Yet they are also given the time and support from university staff to seek out professionals who can help them acquire the skills and knowledge to meet their project's challenges. And because of the team structure of most of the projects, the students can set high goals for themselves knowing that they can rely on their peers to help them develop in areas where they feel most uncomfortable.

Interactive learning

Because creativity cannot be separated from its recognition, one way to inspire creativity is to foster environments that are well suited for the acknowledgement and dissemination of new ideas. The best way to ensure that people push the boundaries of knowledge and identify opportunities for applying their skills creatively is to put them in places where they believe these ideas will actually contribute to change. This is a profound motivating factor, the expectation that one's skills, if put to use in new ways, will make a difference to others.

The programmes we highlight in this report, while diverse in form and structure, all provide examples of environments that not only encourage creative thinking and recognise it as such, but allow for the sharing and implementation of creative ideas. At Unipart, for example, employees participate in problem-solving circles. The products of their efforts are always disseminated and in more cases than not, their ideas are implemented throughout the firm.

At Citizen Schools, student apprentices are not taught that learning occurs in a vacuum. Rather, they always see the fruits of their creativity being put to use. For example, students who studied under a lawyer drafted a law that was put through the Massachusetts State Legislature and another group which apprenticed under an author wrote their own children's books, which are now available in Boston's public library.

The following chapters present case studies of projects and programmes that are exemplars in developing creative ability. They serve different communities and age groups, and have very different aims, but they all excel at fostering environments that encourage and capture the benefits of creativity.

– 4 –

Case studies

The programmes outlined in this chapter are successful in a number of ways. They are all:

- *cultivators of creativity:* learners are encouraged to apply their knowledge and skills in new ways
- *culture changing:* they produce a range of outcomes or products that contribute to the needs of the wider community
- *innovators:* they continuously seek to adapt and improve their programmes in order to meet changing needs of learners
- *visionaries:* they find ways to integrate new educational models with more traditional forms of learning.

In addition, they have all succeeded in achieving the primary mission on which their programmes were based.

- Citizen Schools has increased the number of after-school placements in Boston by 15 per cent and recruited over 1,000 volunteer professionals to teach over 500 learning apprenticeships.
- HEAF has successfully helped 90 per cent of its students gain acceptance into New York City's most competitive high schools. One-hundred per cent of its students have completed high school and gone on to pursue university degrees; this in contrast to the 20 per cent high school degree rate and 10 per cent college degree rate in the surrounding community.
- Hyper Island has helped over 95 per cent of its students gain work in the new media industry upon graduation. The other 5 per cent have gone on to pursue further degrees.
- The University of Waterloo has over 50 per cent of its undergraduates participating in co-operative work placements and has maintained a placement rate of between 93 and 99 per cent per semester. It has been voted

Canada's most innovative university programme and the best single source of tomorrow's leaders in the country.

- In 1996, Unipart increased its profits by over £32 million and it's productivity levels by 30 per cent as a result of its creative learning culture. In 1998, Unipart had its seventh consecutive year of record breaking growth with sales exceeding £1.1 billion. It estimates that in its newer companies at least 30 per cent of its employees are involved in creative problem solving circles with some of their more established factories as high as 100 per cent. Over 1,700 Mark-in Action Awards have been presented to Unipart employees for their outstanding customer service.

Together, these case studies provide powerful insights into how creative ability can be developed in a range of settings.

CITIZEN SCHOOLS

Ned Rimer and Eric Schwarz, co-founders of Boston's Citizen Schools Programme, estimate that children are awake more than 5,000 hours a year. They spend only about 900 to 1,000 of these hours in school, leaving more than 4,000 hours of free time to fill. For most of these children, parental supervision during non-school hours is unlikely. In 1998, more than 13,000 children of working parents in Massachusetts were on the government's waiting list for child care subsidies. Citizen Schools is an out-of-school learning programme for nine to fourteen year olds that aims to use this time as a creative resource.

Those parents who are able to afford out-of-school care are forced to navigate a patchy maze of programmes, few of which provide more than minimal enrichment and supervision. 'We're not looking for board games and television,' US Department of Education Deputy Director for Planning and Evaluation, Adriana Kanter declares, 'we're looking for enriching experiences.'[60] However, for many Boston schoolchildren, the main aim of out-of-school care is custodial.

'Too often,' Schwarz argues, 'the rallying cry is "Let's keep kids off the street." But that's such a low standard. We really need to engage adults from the broader community so that out-of-school time can become one of the highlights of a young child's life. The way kids learn best is by hands-on. And the best people to teach them are experts in those fields.'[61]

The Citizen School movement began in the summer of 1995, with just 50 students and 30 citizen teachers from diverse fields such as journalism, community policing, business, culinary arts and shiatsu massage. Four years and six Citizen School campuses later, the programme has produced a 15 per cent increase in the total number of licensed after-school slots available in Boston.

More than 1,000 volunteer Citizen teachers have now been trained to teach over 521 learning apprenticeships, each culminating in a product or performance that meets community needs. In contrast to the mass of children who spend their free time watching television, playing video games or roaming the streets, student apprentices at Citizen Schools have worked with adult experts to, among other things:

- publish eleven newspapers
- produce three live television shows
- design six web pages
- design and build a networked computer lab from scratch
- start seven profitable businesses
- organise a debate of the Congressional District political candidates attended by 300 people
- file a community service bill in the Massachusetts state legislature
- teach the mayor of Boston how to surf the Internet
- hold nine mock trials in real courtrooms
- write nine children's books now available at the Boston Public Library
- produce eight plays and four dance performances at Boston's First Night Celebration.

In addition to gaining hands-on experience and access to the 'secret terms and technology'[62] of professional domains, Citizens School students participate in a range of sports, team-building activities, and cultural field trips. These activities, while not the primary focus of the programme, are essential to the community-building process and add a sense of adventure to the Citizen School experience. Examples of non-apprentice experiences include climbing the Blue Hills of New Hampshire, milking cows and making ice cream, designing a new sport, solving murder mysteries using 'Sherlock Holmes' style skills and participating in the Citizen Olympics (track) and Citizens Cup (football). During the school year, Citizen School students also use their range of experiences as a basis for developing academic skills such as writing, data analysis and data interpretation.

Learning in the real world

Anyone who has ever taught in the classroom might wonder how a volunteer professional without substantial teacher training convinces a group of children to spend their precious free time learning – as if it isn't hard enough to manage a class of students during regular school hours. But the fact that students are not in school is what seems to drive their learning process.

Take Irvel Sylvestre, a fourteen year old Citizen School apprentice who participated in five after-school apprenticeships during his eighth grade year. According to Irvel, one of the secrets of Citizen Schools success is the opportunity to learn from 'real world' experts. 'The teachers are actually professional,' Irvel explains, 'so it's really neat that they take time out of their work to come and teach us. They have rules, but it is not like they are always telling us what to do, like at school. We can call them by their first names.'[63]

Learning from mistakes

While traditional schools tend to communicate the message that problems can be solved in a matter of minutes, Citizen Schools teaches students like Irvel that real world problems are usually only solved after learning from their mistakes. As an apprentice to a computer technologist, Irvel helped to set up a computer lab in the basement of a school. 'Mine was the fastest,' he says, 'but it ended up not working. They gave me another computer though. [At Citizen Schools] we aren't graded on our mistakes.'[64]

Citizen School students are not constrained by the fear of making mistakes. Just as in the world of work, getting things wrong is often a key to long-term success. Because they are not motivated instrumentally by grades, but by the experience and impact of what they are doing, students are encouraged to view their learning as an incremental process. This belief in progressive learning is essential to their creativity.

Broad-ranging, interactive experience

While students are often categorised as 'artistic' or 'technical' types, Citizen School apprentices experiment with a diversity of professional domains. In doing so, they also exercise 'multiple intelligences', or pathways to learning. For example, to complement his apprenticeship in the field of technology, Irvel became an apprentice in shiatsu massage as well as in dance. Whether or not they latch on to a particular field, apprentices often develop a sense of respect and value for different professions, and begin to value their own contributions. As part of his shiatsu class, Irvel went to a hospital to give the workers free massages. ' I think they liked it,' he reflects back on his contribution, 'they work really long hours.'[65]

Educators are often baffled by how, if students aren't graded, they are motivated to work so hard, especially in their free time? The answer is simply that students want to be there. In contrast to school, apprentices choose what to learn and they see how their hard work makes a difference to others.

'Classes last eight weeks,' Irvel explains, 'which seems like a really long time, but actually it's not. We are always working really hard, but its stuff that we want to do. I like to make sure everything I do is right the first time. We aren't graded, but I like to get things done because there is so much more to do. But it really isn't like school. I hardly even know the time is passing.'[66]

Inventing a new system

Passing time is exactly what Rimer and Schwarz want to avoid. Their vision is of a seamless system which links formal education and after-school child care with school-to-work and community-building. Their goal, as explained by Rimer, is 'changing the way kids grow up in Boston and beyond'. In his view, children should be acknowledged as resources to their community, rather than just burdens.

In addition to their core Citizens Schools programme, Rimer and Schwarz have worked with other educators to design and pilot a 'hands-on' after-school curriculum that teaches writing and problem-solving skills and incorporates local, state and national education standards. They have also teamed up with Boston Public School Office of Instructional Technology to develop a programme that trains students to fix and upgrade computers, and teachers to use the Internet as a pedagogical tool.

Citizen Schools offers a powerful example of how an under-used resource – young people's out-of-school time and attention – can be used to produce multiple gains for schools, families, communities and young people themselves. Rather than treating the school curriculum as a finite resource with fixed boundaries, it has connected formal educational experience with a whole range of other learning opportunities. It offers a number of lessons for developing the creative potential of learners.

Using students as resources

Rather than seeing education as primarily an expense to those who provide it, Citizen Schools see young people as resources with a contribution to make. This is a key to fostering creativity and, as we have seen, to ensuring employability – the double dividend of knowing that what you are doing is having an immediate impact as well as improving your long-term abilities. By making direct contributions to their communities, Citizen Schools students are adding value to their environment as well as to themselves.

Real world domains

Knowledge and learning are structured around the domains and challenges of real life disciplines and professions, rather than around academic subjects or classroom subjects. Students learn massage from masseurs, technology from IT experts, and dance from dancers, and observe the skills being performed at first hand. Students gain access to the 'secret terms and technology' of different domains: insights and understanding which cannot be learned from anything other than direct involvement.

Building networks

Networks are an integral part of the Citizen School approach. Through their experience of apprenticeship, students build up a personal network of support, advice and example, which they can draw on in pursuing their educational goals. Citizen Schools has also created wide-ranging community networks, drawing together diverse community members with a common interest in young people's development. Rimer refers to Citizens Schools teachers and volunteers as 'allies to our school day colleagues'. Part of the key to this relationship is the use of the school as the site for the programme, encouraging connections between those involved in the formal curriculum and those contributing to Citizen Schools. During summer programmes, students are mixed based on interest rather than age, creating what Rimer calls a 'sibling learning' or a 'family culture of learning'.

Developing inter-disciplinary skills

Rather than putting children on a single academic or vocational track, Citizen School has also learned that children need to experience a range of learning opportunities before they are ready to develop a particular career direction. Citizen School offers an age-appropriate opportunity to perform tasks in multiple domains, and gain access to members of diverse fields. It embeds the apprenticeship concept within a community of learning and maintains diverse apprenticeships and recreational activities, so that children don't feel trapped by the idea of one profession or one teacher. Apprenticeships last eight weeks: students can't just give up, but Citizen Schools offers a balance of experimentation and commitment which is crucial during this transitional stage of development. Citizen Schools has the potential to turn a student on to even one profession and provide that student with the confidence, motivation, and most importantly the discipline to focus their attention more effectively at school. The range of learning experiences offered also encourages students to compare and contrast the different domains and disciplines they visit, and to understand the elements that are common to them. This is a vital foundation for building inter-disciplinary skills.

Multiple outcomes and a strong assessment culture

Despite the informal nature of much of the learning in Citizen Schools apprenticeships, detailed assessment is an integral part of the process. Students maintain a 'portfolio' including writing they have produced during the course of a season, data analysis and a record of their apprenticeship. Students present their portfolio to a three to five person panel made up of parents, Citizen Schools staff members and Citizen teachers. They receive feedback on their presentation skills as well as the content of their portfolio. Students also complete self-evaluations and programme evaluations at the end of each Citizen Schools season, which are complemented by parent evaluations and those of citizen teachers. Assessment of what has been achieved over time comes from a range of different perspectives: professional teachers, citizen teachers with specialist expertise, young people, their peers and their parents. This process of multi-dimensional assessment is vital to understanding the different forms of value that learning can generate.

Conclusion

Citizen Schools has shown how whole communities can be used as a creative resource, in order to make more out of time and skills that were previously under-used. It is also an exemplar of new, network based forms of organisation, and shows how new patterns of learning relationship can grow alongside more formal structures. In the process, it is helping to show how students can gain a whole range of skills through highly economical forms of financial investment, while also creating social and cultural value for the communities that they live in.

HARLEM EDUCATIONAL ACTIVITIES FUND

Learning below the poverty line

In 1989 Dan Rose, a successful businessman, decided that too many New York City children were being denied access to good high schools and that without a solid high school education, a college education was an even more remote possibility.

In New York City, where public school students are forced to compete for places in the more academically respected schools, the playing field is far from level. The New York City High School Entrance Placement Exam functions like a demographic sieve, selecting predominantly those who are white and middle class. This is why Dan Rose and his wife Joanna established the Harlem Educational Activities Fund (HEAF), in an effort to help children from Harlem and Washington Heights develop the values, attitudes and skills to lead productive and satisfying lives in 'mainstream' America. In communities where only 20 per cent of residents are high school graduates and less than 10 per cent have college degrees, HEAF's assertion that 'environment is not destiny; all children can learn' has had a profound impact.

HEAF began in 1989, aiming to help prepare eighth-graders to score better on the High School Entrance Placement Examinations. Since then HEAF has grown exponentially, in both size and aspiration. It now recruits students from more than ten schools and provides them with a rich blend of education, youth development and support services, helping them to navigate the range of transitions from seventh grade through to college. Through a combination of experiential learning, rigorous test preparation, skill development and supportive relationships, students are drawn into a way of life. 'As I look toward my college years', one student explains, 'I feel extremely fortunate to have a programme like HEAF to look out for my well-being and growth. My only complaint is that they refuse to let me set up a bed in the office (since I'm here all the time anyway)!'[67]

HEAF pursues a twin track approach to achieving its goals. Alongside rigorous academic training and preparation, it also aims to teach the broader skills and qualities that students will need to thrive in their school settings and beyond. What follows is a description of the HEAF model of success.

Setting 'high expectations'

The first thing that students learn when they join HEAF at the age of eleven is that being a member of the HEAF community means setting high expectations for oneself and for others. The second thing they learn is that to make the successful transition to independent adulthood, they need to believe in themselves and to arm themselves with a wide range of skills, experiences and knowledge. High Expectations is a one-year extended learning programme that inspires and prepares students to compete for places in the top New York City High Schools. While the intended outcome of High Expectations is to increase the numbers of youngsters from disadvantaged backgrounds who attend New York City's more competitive schools, for most students it is just the first leg in a longer path of development.

High expectations: Summer Quest

In 1995, HEAF initiated the Summer Quest Program, a project-based educational simulation to enrich the mathematical and verbal skills of seventh grade (eleven to twelve year old) students. The primary goal of this programme is to motivate high potential students to participate as eighth graders (twelve to thirteen year olds) in HEAF's challenging Test Preparation course and compete for places in top academic secondary schools.

The six week summer programme combines intensive Math and English tutoring with an innovative experiential learning project in which teams of students research, design and prepare business plans for their own restaurant under the guidance of volunteer professionals. Professional mentors are recruited to take part in the summer programme from the fields of restaurant management, culinary arts, architecture, interior design, financing, marketing and consulting. At the end of every summer, three teams of students each present restaurant concepts, menus, marketing strategies, scale models of floor plans and detailed business plans to an audience of parents, teachers, restauranteurs and financiers. In addition to the formal educational value of the Summer Quest curriculum, it has been praised by parents, professional volunteers and education researchers for its ability to motivate and inspire students. 'The thing that I liked most about Summer Quest,' a programme graduate points out 'was that I learned the reason for learning.'[68]

In addition to cultivating a sense of educational purpose and creativity, the Summer Quest experience has shown significant impacts in more academic domains of Math and English. The eighth grade students who attended Summer Quest as seventh graders in 1998 scored 30 points higher than those HEAF students who did not take advantage of the summer sessions before attending the Test Prep course in the fall.

High expectations: Test Prep

Test Prep workshops, held in the fall of eighth grade, prepare students for the High School Entrance Placement examination that is required for admission to the competitive New York City high schools. In 1998, 90 per cent of the students who took this course were accepted into New York City's top academic high schools.

High expectations: Spring into High School

Once HEAF students have taken the placement exams for high school, they prepare for the challenging transition to large, diverse, impersonal high schools. The 'Spring into High School' curriculum provides students with the cognitive, technical, problem-solving and inter-personal skills that will help them to thrive during their secondary school years. Goal-setting, time-management, decision-making, communication, problem-solving, academic preparation, stress-management, inter-familial relations and self-reflection are just a few of the skills that students develop as they gain confidence in 'handling the unknown.'[69]

Every Saturday afternoon for ten weeks, 80 students participate in interactive workshops. Using the metaphor of building a home, the course's curriculum is divided into three interconnected units. 'Laying the Foundation' helps students set a plan and a purpose for their futures and visualise the steps that are required to realise their goals. Goal-setting, prioritising, decision-making, communication, time-management and networking are the skills that form the foundation of this unit and of the environments which they will find themselves in throughout their lives.

'Walls, Rooms and Ceilings' is intended to provide students with 'filling' or insulation to help them to achieve their goals. This unit focuses mainly on academics, family and leisure and encourages students to set boundaries and balance the personal and academic aspects of their lives. Key skills include academic tools such as problem-solving, writing, research, test preparation, self-assessment and studying; inter-personal skills such as communication, soliciting help and setting boundaries in intimate relationships and organisational skills such as identifying extra-curricular interests, and balancing work leisure.

The final workshop series, 'Interior and Exterior Design' focuses on cultivating the students' ability to reflect on their own identity and their place in the world. Developing such skills as stress management, marketing oneself, and making difficult choices around sex and drugs, this unit is designed to help the course graduates gain self-awareness, confidence and self-esteem and to identify the relationship between their own needs, values and personal qualities and those of others.

By the end of the High Expectations programme, students are expected to be 'navigators of their own path',[70] able to manage their academic and personal lives and look confidently towards the future. They have learnt to expect the best from themselves and have been armed with the skills to begin shaping an uncertain and unformed future. Despite the demands on students' time and energy, the High Expectations programme has 85 per cent of its participants staying on right through. The next stage is to support students continuing development through high school.

Providing a 'support net' for success

When HEAF first expanded into the high school years, it was primarily a mentoring programme. The programme was later expanded to include life skills development, tutoring, leadership training, community service, cultural and social enrichment activities, college and personal counselling and parent outreach. HEAF's Support Net programme now has 110 high school students, 78 college students and six full-time staff, fifteen volunteer tutors and over 45 volunteer mentors. Through the four years of high school, HEAF becomes like a home to its students. It is a net on which to fall back, and a network of learning that extends on into college. So far, 100 per cent of the Support Net's high school graduates have gone on to attend college, with no drop-outs to date. Below are the core elements.

Life skills

Every year Support Net students attend a ten session interactive life skills course. The first year of high school focuses on identity and self-reflection, the second year on problem solving and decision-making, the third year on responsibility, career awareness and money management and the final year on independent living and self-reliance.

Academic support

Recognising the need to complement in-school learning with academic remediation and tutoring, HEAF developed biology and English courses for all of their first year students. Students are also expected to take courses in study skills and test preparation. Perhaps most importantly, HEAF monitors students' progress in school and requires subject tutoring for all those who have lower than a 'B' in any subject.

Leadership

Leadership is a theme that finds its way into the daily life of HEAF. The opportunities to serve as a leader within the programme range from a student run newsletter to paid work and a student governance board. HEAF also requires all of its students to attend leadership programmes that provoke reflection on how to be strong leaders in high school and college.

Express Yourself!

Learning to express oneself is an integral aspect of success, happiness and productivity. However, many students tend to fear that in order to master the skills of communication and presentation they will have to repress their own racial or cultural background. HEAF recognises that to reach their full potential, Support Net students need the tools to express themselves with style, clarity and confidence without having to reject their own sense of identity. Equally as important is their ability to interpret and communicate the thoughts and feelings of others.

Every year for ten weeks, Support Net students participate in 'Express Yourself!', an intensive drama programme designed and taught by Denise Woods, a professional actress and the first African-American woman on the faculty of Juilliard, America's most prestigious performing arts academy. Through dramatic drills, practice, readings and improvisations, students learn technical skills such as diction, voice placement and presentation of other skills that are essential to effective communication. In the process, they explore ways to use their voices and bodies to communicate in a range of contexts from college and job interviews to public speaking engagements and personal conflicts. The key to Express Yourself! is that Support Net students are empowered to expand their range of voices and communication skills without having to reject their own racial and cultural identities. 'If I learn well,' one Express Yourself! student points out, 'I'll be able to speak street slang and also speak incredibly proper, I could go to a store like Saks Fifth Avenue, and they'd think I was from London.'[71]

Mentoring

The mentoring programme matches Support Net students with graduate students and college educated professionals. Each student–mentor pair is matched by gender and interests.

Parent involvement

Parent Involvement has been one of HEAF's greatest challenges. As well as a three way agreement signed by parents, students and staff, they have developed various forms of involvement including parent meetings, a parent advisory council and informal social gatherings such as pot luck suppers and programme celebrations.

College Quest and Onward! College

While HEAF is adamant about the importance of cultivating lifelong skills such as the ability to learn and take risks, there is no question that entrance into college is a driving force behind the programme's design. In the first year of high school, they begin with evening workshops for children and parents. This develops into a series of on-site college visits and one-on-one counselling on college selection and financial aid.

The 'College Quest' workshops are instrumental to students' success in the university environment. They develop students' ability to manage personal finances, how to identify and cope with diversity and prejudice and how to mange the delicate balance between work, study and play. Through its 'Onward! College' programme, HEAF continues to provide a network of support through email, phone and regular staff visits. It also offers help with transportation, moving expenses, textbooks, emergency loans and personal computers for all students who maintain a B gradepoint average.

Lessons from HEAF

HEAF is an outstanding example of an environment that cultivates creativity, supporting its students to achieve their goals within education and beyond. It works to harmonise a wide range of theoretical, academic and practical learning experiences with the everyday lives of its members. It provides a number of lessons for policy and practice.

Trust

At HEAF, skills are developed within an atmosphere of trust, openness and support. At the beginning of every programme, students work together to establish a set of ground rules, or norms, such as: agreeing to disagree, being willing to take risks, participating fully in activities, respecting one another and keeping an open mind. The sense of community and mutual trust is reinforced at the beginning of each lesson through interactive 'icebreakers', which help students to let down their guard and remain open to learning. At the end of each HEAF learning activity or set of activities, students always break up into smaller, more intimate 'process circles', where they have the opportunity to reflect back on the dynamics of their group. This gives students a way of stepping back from their learning process in order to maintain self- and interpersonal awareness. It also reminds them that feelings and social interactions can have a vital impact on the way in which they learn.

Combining different kinds of knowledge

Using a climate of trust and support as a basis for all of its learning activities, HEAF then finds ways to blend traditional educational mediums such as literature or documentaries with more personal pathways to learning. For example, senior students learning about diversity start out one of their 'lessons' by reading an excerpt from a piece of literature and reflecting on the meaning of that excerpt. They then move on to a set of case studies about racism on college campuses and ultimately use one of their own personal experiences as a basis for discussion and reflection. What starts out looking like an English class will slowly transform into a very personalised discussion about how to address racism in their own lives.

This blend of theoretical and experiential learning pervades all of HEAF's programmes. For example, students who participate in HEAF's renowned chess programme (HEAF's chess students have been national chess champions for three out of the programme's nine years) rely on their passion for chess as a pathway for learning scientific principles such as matter and mass, or geographical principles such as longitude and latitude. This blended approach encourages students to apply what they learn in school to their own lives, and helps them to see how their own lives can serve as a bridge towards understanding concepts they are taught in school. They are constantly called upon to apply what they know over time as they engage in progressive problem-solving.

Progression over time

Another key element is the provision of opportunities to develop and build on skills over time. Whilst students in the traditional classroom are usually taught that skills and knowledge can be learned, tested and put to rest, HEAF students are constantly revisiting their skill sets, applying them in different domains and at different stages of their lives. Take goal-setting for example. While HEAF makes a concerted effort to expose students to goal-setting and evaluation techniques, it is careful not to 'teach' students that these are discrete skills which can be learned in a 'lesson' or two. If you ask a HEAF student what goals she set for herself while participating in HEAF, the most likely response would be 'what kind of goals?', 'which aspect of my life?' or 'at what point in my life?'.

Students at HEAF are repeatedly called on to articulate what they know, what they don't know and what they feel they should know. Many of the programme components cultivate the self-management, self-awareness and communication skills that help students to adapt as they cross temporal, geographical, intellectual and cultural boundaries. By the time a HEAF student reaches the brink of adulthood, she has the self-awareness and confidence to thrive in virtually any environment.

Measuring different outcomes differently

HEAF is explicitly aimed at boosting the formal educational success of its students. Since qualifications and college are such important determinants of their life chances, it takes grades and exams very seriously. But it aims to develop a far wider range of skills. How do they know what to measure?

HEAF does not rely on decontextualised measures of soft skill development. Instead, competencies such as problem-solving, leadership, teamwork and communication are embedded in the full range of activities. Rather than grading students on what they have learned in their life skills workshops, HEAF expects its students to apply what they have learned in the course of their participation in required activities. According to Courtney Welsh, HEAF's Executive Director, part of the reason they have chosen not to grade students on their performance in each of the skill areas they teach is that 'kids become very adept at telling you what you want to know'.

In schools, it is not just teachers who learn how to 'teach to the test'. Students know how to 'learn to the test' as well, whether it is an essay or a lab experiment. In effect, one of the skills we are best at teaching students is how to predict what educators want from them. This is one of the problems with relying on entirely decontextualised forms of assessment. We assume that when a student is able to demonstrate his grasp of a skill on a test, or an essay, or even in one real life context, that surely he must know how to apply this skill in any context which he so chooses. But HEAF is not satisfied by single performances. It requires its students to use what they have learned throughout their time, and in a wide diversity of simulated and real contexts.

Take for example, problem-solving. Students at HEAF are first introduced to this skill when they join Summer Quest and spend their summer designing a business plan. They practice the skill of problem-solving repeatedly throughout the summer, as they try to decide what type of restaurant will succeed with their specific market, or how much financing they will need from the bank to start-up and maintain their business. Later, as sophomores in high school, they take a ten week course on problem-solving and decision-making. Again they will be asked to solve problems, many of which are based on case studies that previous HEAF students have designed.

But the key to measuring success in problem-solving is calling upon students to solve real problems that occur during their tenure. For example, HEAF found that the male drop-out rate in its programme was rising and was deeply concerned about how to reverse the trend. Rather than bringing in consultants to offer expert opinions, HEAF planned a weekend retreat with all of its male staff and students. This was their problem to solve, and they had two full days to debate, reflect and come up with a proposal for change. The proposal was filled with creative solutions, such as the need to change the mentoring programme so that it was more developmentally appropriate. It was felt that peers were very important to younger boys and that they would gain more from sharing an adult mentor than from having a one-on-one relationship.

Alongside formal academic performance, HEAF therefore monitors and evaluates a wide range of other outcomes. Many of them are based on the impact of learning on real life, whether for individual students or the wider community. Students are integrally involved in assessing these outcomes and working out how to improve them. This variation of context and diversity of types of outcome is essential to the process of creative development.

Continuous support for high expectations

Because students are expected to participate fully in HEAF's programmes, HEAF focuses particular attention on those who fail to get involved. Non-involvement or problematic involvement is an indicator that students may need extra support in developing and refining some skills. The forum for such reflection is a weekly case management meeting in which all HEAF staff come together to discuss any 'outliers' who are struggling with the daily requirements of membership. This approach is not independently capable of measuring with accuracy the 'softer' capacities of its students, so HEAF is working to develop a list of day to day behavioural indicators that skills are being used, so that all students can be observed more closely and with more clarity. This form of monitoring, which takes underperformance as a trigger for closer attention and support, rather than a personal failure of commitment or responsibility, is an essential part of the environment which HEAF seeks to create.

Conclusion

Yasmin Moya is entering her final year at Bryn Mawr, a renowned women's college. She has just finished studying urban development for six months at London City College and plans to return to Harlem after graduation to start her own community-based credit union. Being part of the HEAF community during her transition from childhood to youth and adulthood has not only put her on the road to academic and personal success, but has also helped her to imagine an infinite world of roads she might like to travel down. Yasmin explains,

'As a junior at Bryn Mawr College I can now see the many (with many still to come) fruits of HEAF's labours. The tutoring, the leadership and the life management workshops, and the mental and emotional support I have received have all played an enormous role in my ability to see more clearly what it is I need, what I want, what it is I really do not need. And it has given me the courage and wisdom to accurately assess the significance of my wants.'

HEAF is a reflection of its students' lives, rather than a programme which they are slotted into. It offers a powerful vision of what a creative environment should look like, of a place where every learner has high expectations of themselves and of others, and where they are constantly learning to apply what they know, and what they do not know, to any situation they might encounter in life.

HYPER ISLAND

When Jonathon Briggs, David Erixon and Lars Lundh came up with the idea for the Hyper Island School of New Media Design, they envisioned an environment where students could learn the new media trade in much the same way that one learns to ride a bike. They believed that good learning experiences always involve trying, failing and trying again until everything suddenly clicks into place. They also wanted students to graduate from a programme that gave them a holistic education, one that didn't divorce the concept of schooling from that of working, or the 'technical' process of design technology from the business management side of the trade. All their students, they agreed, should graduate with a 'helicopter's view' of what it takes to manage, co-ordinate and take part in new media projects. While their graduates would perform a whole range of roles within the new media industry, they would leave Hyper Island with the ability to 'speak the same language' and to recognise that their professional interdependence is the key to lifelong learning.

Briggs, Chief Executive of 'theothermedia' and Professor of New Media Design, had taught Erixon at Kingston University in 1997 and Lundh, a former politician and entrepreneur had subsequently employed Erixon as a project manager at his film production company in Stockholm. Together, the three men incorporated their educational vision in the hopes that they could implement a programme that would fuse the traditional split between academic and vocational learning. When the Swedish government announced its plan to start new vocational universities throughout Sweden, Briggs, Erixon and Lundh applied for funding to operate their two-year course in Karlskrona, an ex-naval town, now referred to by the Swedes as 'Telecom City'.

Just as one is more likely to learn the art of bike riding from an experienced bike rider, the founders of Hyper Island were committed to using the experienced professional as a teacher of new media design. In 1996, the first 'crew' of 45 Hyper Island students, or 'Hypernauts', arrived in Telecom City for a two-year experiment in learning. Their home was an old prison that had been renovated by Lundh and equipped with state-of-the-art new media facilities. Their campus, however, would stretch as far as San Francisco, New York, London and Oslo.

The design of Hyper Islands' two-year course not only represents a unique alternative to traditional new media programmes, it offers a glimpse into the future of all university schooling.

Inter-disciplinary teaching and learning

In contrast to the academic divisions that define traditional university programmes, Hyper Island offers its students an opportunity to learn within an inter-disciplinary framework that blends teaching and assessment strategies from business, technology and design. The courses are planned and taught by Hyper Island staff and professionals from diverse fields and nationalities to reflect the range of skills and knowledge involved in the execution of 'real world' projects. Students are expected (both in the classroom and during their industrial placements) to apply their skills and knowledge across disciplinary boundaries, so that they graduate with the ability to work in and manage multi-functional teams. As explained by student Thomas Langvik, 'At Hyper Island we get encouraged to try and take responsibility for areas that we might not feel comfortable with.' This process gives students more 'insight into the different work roles that exist in a project and makes us better project managers.'[72]

Learner-centred, problem-based learning

According to programme director Rebecca Lindberg, it is the students at Hyper Island who drive the learning process. At Hyper Island, she explains, 'we provide an environment for learning, we don't feed you like a bird.' While there are lectures and presentations given by school staff and lecturers from the New Media profession, the bulk of students' work involves individual and group responsibility for projects that can last anywhere from one day to six weeks. All of these projects are formulated around industry-related problems and products and, in many cases, students take part in 'live projects' that are commissioned globally by firms from the new media industry.

While there is a core curriculum of coursework, students often determine for themselves where there are gaps in their knowledge and how to fill them. Sometimes this means bringing professionals into the classroom and often it means venturing out into the 'real world' to find solutions to their problems. This is what Hyper Island staff refer to as a problem-based learning approach, one which integrates theory and practice into each subject and project. The role of the teacher at Hyper Island is to serve as a guide or mentor, as the students work individually and in teams to manage their own projects. Each project results in skills, knowledge and experiences that form the foundation of the next project, creating an educational 'development chain'. This chain, in turn, generates in students a sense of responsibility for their own educational development and helps them to transfer what they have learned across time and context.

As student Lukas Mollersten says, students are taught to see the learning process as incremental and to recognise their own role in identifying the desired outcomes of their learning.

'Most of the knowledge I've gained isn't static or "plain facts". It's more like some seed of knowledge has been given to me and now it's up to me what I want to do with it, how I feed it and make it grow. You could call it problems for me to solve ... The bottom line is that it's not about what the school expects from me its more about what I expect from myself.'[73]

As in the world of work, success is not earned through conformity, but through independent thinking, effective management of time and resources, and willingness to take risks. At Hyper Island, student Maria Andersson explains, 'you are taught and encouraged to do things differently and experiment with odd designs ... there are no right and wrong answers on how we solve problems and answer questions.'[74]

Perhaps most importantly, Hyper Island's signature approach to problem-based learning highlights the essential role of the audience in cultivating creative learners. Marking is based on production for a real audience. Students learn to evaluate each other's work through the peer marking process and they also learn to evaluate their own work using 'real world' criteria as they periodically participate in 'live projects'. When asked how work is assessed and judged at Hyper Island, former student Karl Andersson points out that the outcomes are captured as students build up a portfolio of genuine products, many of which have been generated while working in the field. Hyper Island, he believes, is like a 'two-year interview'. However, knowledge to a Hypernaut is only as valuable as its latest application. In the real world, and at Hyper Island, graduate Mattias Nystrom explains 'you're never better than your last project'.

Learning networks

Hyper Island is a model for the twenty-first century university partly because it seeks to improve on the notion of a two to four-year 'degree' by cultivating learning networks that will last a lifetime. For most Hypernauts, making connections across individual and organisational boundaries is an unconscious part of every day life. Reflecting back on his two years at Hyper Island, Karl Andersson explains that 'networking is a skill that we learned without knowing it.' To the outsider, it is clear that a number of mechanisms form the backbone of Hyper Island's 'lifelong' university.

First, Hypernauts realise early on that some of the most valuable learning occurs when working collaboratively with others. While students complete individual projects and maintain an ongoing portfolio of work, the production group is the primary means of teaching what work will be like in the 'real world'. Within these collaborative teams, students are able to develop their communication, co-operation and leadership skills, all of which are integral to the ongoing maintenance of learning networks.

Throughout the course of a project, production groups will encounter a range of setbacks, many of which are laced with emotional, rather than intellectual differences. One of the main responsibilities of Hyper Island staff is to encourage students to step back from group endeavors and discuss the inter-personal undercurrents that affect their collaborative efforts. By regularly processing their group experiences and identifying their own role within this micro-network, students develop the communicative and reflective capacities to make the most of learning networks in the future. Student Thomas Langvik explains,

> 'We have a feeling of unity in our class that contributes to the success of our projects. We are taught to help each other to see our work in different perspectives by giving each other constructive criticism.'

Using the production group as a foundation for network learning, Hyper Island students are then challenged to apply the skills they have learned within the professional world. For twenty weeks, Hypernauts participate in industrial placements at firms they have chosen to match their specific career interests. These placements mark the expansion of their learning network beyond school boundaries and serve as an opportunity to take the lead in determining from whom they would like to learn.

Most of us who have attended secondary school or university would have difficulty naming more then ten classmates with whom we still maintain contact. If you ask a Hyper Island graduate who has remained a part of their personal and/or professional circle, the answer is likely to be 'everyone'. This is due in large part to the creation of a Hyper Island Internet database, which was designed by a group of students last year to serve as a lifeline to the larger learning network that makes up the Hyper Island community.

'www.hyperisland.se' is probably one of the most powerful Internet addresses in new media design. It is also a testament to the success of Hyper Island in cultivating learning networks that extend well beyond the two years that students spend together in Karlskrona. Not only is this virtual community used as a hyper 'plaza', where students come together to have virtual conversations and catch up on each others lives, it is also a media centre where news can be broadcast, a marketplace where jobs can be advertised and sought out, and a 'university' where knowledge can be generated and exchanged.[75] Through this site, students can search through individually updated descriptions of each student's own personal interests, career experience and knowledge-base in order to see who knows about what. They can also communiate with people in the new media industry and with Hyper Island lecturers who want to offer their advice or knowledge to students and graduates who may need it. Reflecting on Hyper Island's virtual network Nystrom says, 'there's not a single person who can't learn anything from someone else.' Andersson adds, 'It's the only real resource I use, it's become a proper community.'

How does Hyper Island know it is successful?

It is not just the graduates who are confident in the value of a Hyper Island diploma, but the people who hire Hypernauts upon graduation. Ninety-five per cent of its students find work within the New Media Industry upon graduation and the others have gone on to further study. Aside from this indicator of its success, how does Hyper Island know that it has succeeded in cultivating the skills and knowledge that make for creative, lifelong learners?

The creative environment

Hyper Island takes the perspective that an essential part of assessing a student's academic and personal capacities is also assessing the environment in which he or she is asked to perform. For this reason, all Hyper Island students evaluate the effectiveness of teaching at the school. Unlike many educational contexts, where students feedback to an administration, student evaluations of the teaching and content at Hyper Island drive the way the programme is structured from year to year. Not only do they influence how classes and sets of skills are taught, but also which skills are taught and which professionals are brought in to serve as Hyper Island teachers in the future. This approach recognises the role of environment in determining what students learn. It provides a richly textured picture of how and why students succeed or fail in developing new skills and applying what they already know.

A culture of cross-evaluation

Students at Hyper Island also evaluate their own and each other's work. Every product a team or an individual creates is evaluated by at least two other individuals or teams, and students are required to spend a minimum of 30 minutes on each evaluation. Jonathan Briggs, a professor with many years experience of judging students work, points out that teachers and professors are often assumed to be the most objective critics of students' work. Yet, when spending hours on end judging the work of 30 or more students, it is common for teachers to change their standards as they progress through the grading process. Some teachers become more critical markers as they realise that what they thought was an 'A' pales in comparison to the work of others. Some relax standards as they realise that their criteria may have been too harsh. Despite the supposed objectivity of assessment based on predetermined criteria, many teachers would willingly admit that they rarely have the time to gain a holistic impression of an entire group's work before setting about the grading process.

Hyper Island's answer to this problem is that students should be assured that their work will be judged based on the thoughtful reflections of a wider field of 'experts', including peers, teachers and the professionals who may have profited from the projects they produce. They also deserve to be assessed by people who have the time to give them ample feedback on the quality of their work.

Peer marking not only benefits the students whose skills are being assessed. Evaluation of oneself and others is a critical skill in today's world, for it helps one to be a more creative learner. Hyper Island recognises the value of evaluation and has intentionally designed its programme to provide opportunities to demonstrate this skill in ways that genuinely matter. Hypernauts carry enormous responsibility. Their judgements over the course of their two years will impact on their peers' records of achievement, their own record of achievement and on the employment of the professionals who are brought in to teach at Hyper Island.

Skills are also measured informally at Hyper Island. In particular, skills such as communication, teamwork, leadership and problem-solving are assessed regularly as students are brought together to process their experiences in the classroom. During these regular periods of reflection students are asked to put aside their thoughts, feelings and ideas about the content of their coursework so that they can reflect on the inter-personal and intrapersonal aspects of learning. These regular sessions are facilitated by Hyper Island Staff and employees of 'Ett Helt Liv' (a whole life), an organisation that specialises in soft skill development. Together they help students to shed light on each other's skills and qualities without the pressure of being formally evaluated.

Combining forms of knowledge

Essential to Hyper Island's success as an accredited programme is that it does not entirely reject the notion of grading. It simply widens the field of experts who take part in the grading process and integrates more decontextualised forms of assessment such as exams with context-based measures of performance, such as the 'live project'. It is no surprise that so many students are hired immediately upon graduation, as those familiar with Hyper Island know that its students have the ability to learn new skills and knowledge as well as the ability to apply these within a diversity of environments. Two years at Hyper Island gets you far more than a diploma. 'I walked away with knowledge,' Nystrom declares assuredly, 'rather than a paper saying that I have knowledge'.

Conclusion

Hyper Island provides a model of the twenty-first century university. It is organised around a cluster of specialised knowledge – the 'New Media' – and facilitates both in-depth specialist knowledge and broader multi-disciplinary skills. It fuses together different kinds of skill development, relating technical and content-based knowledge to the needs of users and creating enduring relationships between students, professionals and mentors. It provides the space and time for experimentation and failure, but relates learning explicitly to the demands and opportunities of the workplace. It relies heavily on networks as a form of organisation and has created a network that spans far beyond its current students and location. It gives learners a formative role in the shaping their own environment and relies on diverse but complementary forms of assessment to evaluate the different kinds of outcomes that its courses produce.

UNIVERSITY OF WATERLOO

In 1957, the Faculty of Engineering at University of Waterloo pioneered the first Canadian co-operative education programme. Seventy-five men were given the opportunity to complement their academic studies with hands-on experience in the field of engineering. Forty years later, over 130 colleges and universities in Canada have followed Waterloo's lead by implementing the co-operative approach to learning. Waterloo continues to lead the pack. A 1992 survey of 2,000 of Canada's opinion leaders concluded that the University of Waterloo was the most innovative programme and the best single source of tomorrow's leaders in the country – due in large part to the fact that over 50 per cent of its undergraduate students were involved in co-operative learning.[76]

Each year approximately 10,000 Waterloo students in over 80 co-op programmes (spread over six teaching faculties) spend anywhere from four to eight months applying and building on their knowledge and skills while working in the 'real world'. By the time a typical co-op student graduates, he or she will have had the equivalent of from sixteen months to two years of full-time work experience, and exposure to more working environments than most have had by the time they reach 30. There are a number of reasons why Waterloo is viewed as a hotbed for creativity and leadership.

Rotation of learning

In contrast to more conventional internship or apprenticeship programmes that last six months to a year, Waterloo students have the opportunity to alternate regularly between academic study on campus and work in course-related jobs. Each 'school' year is twelve months long, with students alternating between four month work terms and four months of academic study. This work-learn-work approach allows students to transfer skills and knowledge across the academic–vocational divide, with each new experience influencing the choices they make in the future.

According to Cathie Jenkins, Associate Director of (Co-operative Education) Programme Services, the school encourages employers to hire students based on 'what they can do, not what they have done in the past.' When students know that they are more likely to be hired for their potential rather than their specific academic or work experience, they have the freedom to be professionally adventurous. The rotating work-learn-work cycle that Waterloo has pioneered allows its students to experience a range of career roles and environments, rather than confining them to one 'apprenticeship' path. This can have life changing implications for students.

Take for example, Jennifer Candlish, a University of Waterloo nominee for the 1998 Canadian Association for Co-operative Education 'Student of the Year' award. Jennifer entered university as an Applied Health Sciences student, intending to go on to medical school. After completing a range of work experiences with Chatham-Kent Community Care Access Centre, Health Canada and Baxter Corporation, and incorporating what she learned into her academic experience, Jennifer's career goals shifted. Instead of being a doctor, she decided to pursue a career in health education and health promotion. This decision, in turn, influenced her choice to complete her most recent work term in Ghana as a health services volunteer for Canadian Crossroads International.[77] This cyclical process of action and reflection provides invaluable opportunity to develop a sense of self-awareness. Equally as important is that a process of risk-taking, experimentation and lifelong learning is set in motion. For those students who remain true to their original career path, the processes of networking and role experimentation on the job at the very least challenge them to move beyond the traditional skill sets that comprise their area of study.

Building networks

It is not just host employers that make up the networks cultivated by co-op students, but also the people they meet in connection with their work responsibilities. Bipasha Choudhury's experiences as a co-op student included: working as a Commercial Officer Intern for the Foreign Trade Office in Taiwan; working in the Department of Foreign Affairs in Ottawa as a Project Analyst in the Trade Department division for Central and Eastern Europe; and serving as the Social Development Officer for the former Department of the Secretary of State of Canada.

Not only did these work experiences help Bipasha develop and refine her communication and networking skills, they also created new opportunities for expanding her professional network and applying what she had learned in the field. This year she was appointed as a member of 'Team Canada', a federal trade mission led by Prime Minister Jean Chretien in which she helped increase business between Canada and South Korea, Thailand and the Phillipines.[78]

In some cases, the networks that co-op students tap into lead to more permanent employment. For example, as a student in Waterloo's Environmental Studies programme, Tom Arnold spent a term working at the Churchill Northern Studies Centre, a non-profit organisation that facilitates arctic research and education. One of the guests who took part in one of Tom's presentations was so persuaded by his presentation that he offered Tom a job with his environmental consulting group upon graduation.[79]

Concrete outcomes

One of the biggest gaps in traditional education is the absence of purpose that students feel when their learning makes no impact on those around them. Dan Pronovost is a graduate of Waterloo's co-operative education programme and an employee of one of its host employers, Joint Technology Corporation. As someone who has experienced co-operative learning from both the student and the employer perspective, he recognises that the co-operative experience is not a substitute for a good education, but rather 'a complement'. Yet he also feels strongly that when you add purpose to the academic experience, 'the learning potential is colossal.'

A great deal of the potential for learning at Waterloo stems from the innate need students have to engage in work that is meaningful to others. Philip Corriveau, of the Industry of Canada's Communications Research Centre (CRC) has been hiring Waterloo students from the psychology department for years because he thinks they are 'innovative and fresh thinking'. But while some Waterloo students may be creative learners before they enter university, it is the repeated opportunity to make a difference that unleashes the creative potential of most students. One of Corriveau's co-op students, Bronwen Hughes, explains that her decision to return to CRC for a second work term was not only based on the technical skills that she was able to develop there. It was also because the staff 'made students feel a part of the team, not like temporary employees.' The sense that one is an integral part of a larger community is not just about the way one is treated by others, but also about the way one's work is validated and shared. After one term at CRC, Bronwen is already a published author.[80]

What's in it for industry?

While it is easy to see how Waterloo's programme has tangible educational and economic benefits for its students, the advantages for host employers are not quite as straightforward. Waterloo has high expectations of its host employers. They encourage extensive supervision, training and mentoring as well as ongoing student evaluation. And unlike interns, who may work for little or nothing in order to get a career start, Waterloo co-op students can be more expensive. In many cases, students are paid rather well, as the employers know that they are competing with hundreds of other potential hosts, also vying for the best students.[81] In fact, most students pay their way through university with the funds they earn during their work terms, as did Dan Pronovost. While Pronovost confesses that the co-op programme is more expensive for students, he believes it is well worth the extra cost. It functions, he says, 'like its own little company', one which successfully places between 94 to 98 per cent of co-op applicants each term.

Incentives for investment

But what exactly do employers get in exchange for their willingness and often eagerness to invest in young, temporary workers?

The answer is that the success of Waterloo's partnership approach is supported by a system of incentives that Ontario's provincial government has implemented to boost the co-operative model of education. The Co-operative Education Tax Credit (CETC) and the Graduate Transitions Tax Credit (GTTC) reimburse businesses that hire co-op students or graduates at a rate of 10 to 15 per cent of salaries and wages, including taxable benefits. The maximum CETC available for each qualifying co-operative education work term is $1,000 and the maximum GTTC available is $4,000 for each new hire.

Aside from the financial incentive to invest in the knowledge and skills development of young, temporary workers, companies are primarily motivated by the opportunity to evaluate potential employees without any long-term obligation. They also have access to low-cost workers (compared to permanent, full-time employees), many of whom have already had a wide range of work experiences through Waterloo's programme.[82]

Some of Waterloo's host employers have come to realise that they can protect their investment in co-op students by creating their own system of incentives for these potential employees. Joint Technology Corporation (JTC), for example, the Waterloo-based software company where Dan Pronovost works, developed an innovative programme to attract talented co-op students back to the firm as full-time employees. Those students who perform to exceptional standards during their work term at JTC receive company stock options that mature while the students are in school. These options can be earned over the course of single or multiple work terms and may be 'cashed-in' if and when they accept an offer for full-time employment with the firm after graduation.

Edward Lam was one of the first students to work for JTC as a software developer, as well as the first to benefit from the company's innovative stock option programme. Not surprisingly, he chose to return to the firm for his final work term at Waterloo. While the stock option programme was a partial motivator in his decision to return to JTC, the sense of self-efficacy and belonging that he gained as a company employee was the primary impetus for his return. 'You feel more motivated because they respect you and trust you, making you feel important. The stock options are a symbol, they show you how the company treats you.'[83]

There is an important lesson to be learned from the co-operative students at the University of Waterloo. In the twenty-first century, economic incentive will not be the only thing that ensures loyalty in the midst of uncertainty. In the case of Waterloo, it is the firms that provide the most creative environments that attract the students time and time again. Where there are opportunities to network, expand one's skills, explore new territory and make a difference to others, there will always be creative learners.

Measuring success

Alongside academic course grades, the co-operative programme uses a range of other instruments to evaluate a student's progress. For each work term, the employer provides an evaluation of on-the-job performance in the following areas:

- communication (written and verbal)
- interpersonal behaviour
- dependability
- problem-solving skills
- creativity
- judgement
- ability to learn
- quality of work
- response to supervision
- leadership qualities
- planning and organising skills
- initiative
- interest in work.

All evaluations are based on the context-specific judgement of a particular employer, ranging from unsatisfactory to outstanding and based on the specific goals and challenges of the work term. While individual employer evaluations are confidential, students can choose to share them with potential employers.

Some employers ask students to fill out the same evaluation forms as their supervisors so that they can use them as a basis for reflection and discussion. However, the ultimate evaluations of their performance on the job come from their supervisors. At the end of each work term, students have a return-to-campus interview with one of 35 field co-ordinators. The feedback given to co-ordinators helps them to advise future employers about how to make the most of the co-operative learning experience. Students can also fill in work term summaries of the pros and cons of their host organisation, so that their peers have a database of information that can help them to make decisions about where to apply for work in the future. Students must complete a minimum of four work reports (one per term) that, for most programmes, are marked by both an on-campus evaluator and the employer.

Over time, every student also develops a work term 'Co-op History' compiled by the university, which includes the names of the companies where they have worked, their job titles and their overall grades.

Developing suitable work opportunities is a notoriously difficult process for most education institutions. Persuading employers to take students on, matching the right people to the right opportunities and ensuring that the experience is productive and fulfilling can be a mammoth task. Yet Waterloo has created a system that achieves placement rates of over 95 per cent and has won acclaim from students, employers and educators. Waterloo graduates are among the most sought after in the new media, information technology and creative industries. Their success as creative learners is measured not just by their degree class, but by their ability to integrate academic knowledge with practical experience and to contribute to real life problems and projects while they continue to develop their abilities.

Waterloo has shown that effective new combinations of work and learning can be created even within traditional university settings. A series of complementary innovations have made it possible to organise high-quality placements for practically all of its students and to make practical creativity and skills application an integral part of higher education. The elements include:

- a well-developed brokerage service that maintains links with employers, matches individual students with appropriate employment opportunities and markets the programme to potential employers
- a system of assessment that combines employer, student and academic perspectives
- an innovative course structure that supports students to integrate on-the-job experience with academic study and allows opportunities to try a range of different work environments
- a form of subsidy that provides incentives to employers to invest in students and helps to spread investment in learning between government, the individual and the employer.

UNIPART GROUP OF COMPANIES

According to Unipart Group's Chief Executive, John Neill, 'People cannot be forced to learn and innovate, but within the right context, they can be encouraged to do so.'[84] In 1987, Neill and his colleagues set out to redesign their manufacturing firm so that creative learning would grow naturally from the environment. At Unipart, creativity is not taken for granted as a matter of genetic heritage, individual motivation or even external compulsion. Their goal is neither to hire 'creative people', nor to rely on chance. Frank Nigriello, Director of Corporate Affairs, says, 'Innovation is not a bit of serendipity'.

It is not just one or two managers who take seriously the role of environment in influencing the creative potential of individuals. It's not even one or two departments. At Unipart, creativity seems to come naturally – not because employees are expected to take a course on creativity and problem-solving, but because there is virtually nowhere in the life of the firm where creative learning is set aside. It pervades Unipart's physical environment and its staff relationships, and it defines the company's distinctive approach to professional and personal development.

Life at Unipart

If you walked into Unipart's headquarters without any prior knowledge of the company, you could walk the entire ground floor of the building and still not know what type of work the firm specialises in. The environment has been carefully designed to communicate the message that working at Unipart does not mean leaving the rest of your life behind you when you come through the doors each day. To the left of the Unipart welcome desk is Unipart U, the company's in-house university. In contrast to many firms that outsource training programmes, Unipart U is strategically located at the heart of the firm. This, Nigriello says, is to demonstrate the company's commitment to continuous learning. 'We haven't built a training centre at the end of the car park so people can go there once a year when they're unlucky.'

In the centre of Unipart U, you'll find an airy window-lined café, a plant-filled library, a computer centre, a health and fitness centre complete with squash courts and a series of bright and comfortable conference rooms. Even the walls at Unipart are considered to be an integral factor in supporting the creative learner. John Neill intentionally lined the library and the IT centre with glass walls to make them more visible and inviting to employees.

While the company has received accolades for its extensive in-house university, the entire building serves as a company campus. Employees may spend free time in the 'Lean Machine' with a company fitness instructor or in 'The Orchard' with a nutritionist, exploring ways to enhance their physical well-being. Or perhaps they will find their way to the library, where they can catch up on the news or check out a book on business management.[85] Some will find their way to the 'The Leading Edge' (Unipart's IT training centre) where they can try out the latest software without having to buy it first[86] or they may work with an IT instructor to upgrade their technology skills. Some will wander into the 'Internet Discovery Centre' where they can surf the web or click into Unipart's Virtual Business Park, its new on-line university. Others will be building their skills and knowledge without having to leave the shop floor, as Unipart has equipped all its shop floors with the latest technology and learning devices, otherwise referred to as its 'faculty on the floor'. Not only has Unipart tried to infuse learning into the daily life of its staff, it also encourages its employees to make learning part of their home life. Classes are often given for families on-site, particularly in the area of IT, and staff are allowed to check out books and lap-tops as well as software packages from its IT library.

Even the courses offered by the university – courses that develop the technical, personal and leadership skills of company employees – are flexibly designed to accommodate the learning needs of employees. There is no 'chalk and talk' at Unipart U, according to Nigriello and Ian Campbell, Director of Unipart's Advance Learning Systems Department. All the classes are designed to be experiential and hands-on, so that staff stay engaged. 'It ain't school', Nigriello says, as if to assure that Unipart U has intentionally planned its curriculum and methodology to redefine the learning process. 'We had to make the university compelling because a lot of people who worked for us had been failed by the education system ... [which] seemed to almost program them for failure.'

Unipart's coursework is based on the belief that too many companies and educational institutions teach skills and knowledge without providing ample opportunities to apply them. 'We don't train people so that only 20 per cent of what people get is value-added', Nigriello explains. The goal, adds Campbell, is to break skills and knowledge down into 'bite-sized chunks' so that people can demonstrate and practice what they've learned right away, rather than lose what they have gained because new skills and knowledge remain dormant over time. Evidence suggests that this more compact learn-then-work approach is a much more effective means of skill development, as training programmes have shown minimal impact when not timed appropriately and followed up soon afterwards at work.[87]

Working and learning for a 'shared destiny'

In 1987, when Unipart became independent from the transportation group British Leyland, Neill led the dramatic shift from an adversarial to a stakeholder model of working relationships. 'We must create shared destiny relationships with all of our stakeholders; customers, employees, suppliers, governments and the communities in which we operate.'[88] Put into practice, Neill's vision of 'shared destiny' has evolved into deep and far-reaching learning networks within and beyond the organisation. These networks provide a twenty-first century image of 'learning beyond the classroom',[89] relying on a broad range of resources to ensure lifelong learning.

The first type of lifelong learning network that Unipart has come to embody is that of the inter-organisational network. Unlike many companies, which define themselves in opposition to their local and global competitors, Unipart has set a standard of inter-organisational learning and mutual alliance. For example, Neill and a group of Unipart Group employees went to Japan back in 1987 to learn how one of its customers, Honda, worked in co-operation with one of their suppliers, Yachiyo. The goal was to learn as much as possible about how to transform competitive, win-lose relationships into stakeholder relationships, where problems are solved for the mutual benefit of all parties. Interestingly, just nine years later, Unipart, Honda and Yachiyo joined forces in a £35 million deal to form a new manufacturing company based on commercial and creative interdependence.

A second type of shared destiny has evolved in the form of a Unipart intra-organisational learning network, the central component of which is the OCC (Our Contribution Counts) circle. The OCC circle is an adaptation of what Unipart learned from studying Japanese and American 'quality circle' programmes and involves cross-functional teams that come together to improve work processes and produce innovations. While all employees take a course at Unipart U in the skill of problem-solving, most of the skill development in this area comes from real life practice of working collaboratively with peers. Whenever a Unipart employee discovers an opportunity to solve a problem, he or she registers his intention with the company and pulls together an OCC team. If solving the problem requires the cultivation of new skills, employees are encouraged to seek out formal training through the university as well as informal training through their colleagues. The OCC team then agrees on a set of goals, acquires sponsorship from management and has three months to report its progress. Once the goals are reached, the team is automatically dissolved.

The creative learning that takes place during this process is by no means confined to the members of the OCC teams. In order to disseminate innovative ideas and products, Unipart has set up a website on its intranet that is entirely dedicated to the knowledge generated by its creative learners. There is also a formal recognition process (see next section).

While creativity on the job is certainly a priority, Unipart also recognises that the life skills and personal interests of it's employees are fundamental to maintaining a creative learning network and to the long-term employability of their staff. This is why Unipart U offers a range of courses such as their creativity workshop, which helps employees to 'step outside their comfort zone'[90] and access their creative core through artistic mediums such as pottery, dance and painting. The university also offers a life skills course that teaches employees how to thrive in a world defined by 'certainty of change'.[91] Using a range of neurolinguistic programming techniques, the course helps people to identify their own patterned reactions to change and create more productive ways of managing uncertainty.

The impact of Unipart U's programmes on the personal and working lives of company employees has inspired the firm to expand beyond the manufacturing industry and market its creative know-how. As the 'student body' of Unipart U expands to include community members, government officials and businesses throughout the world, another model of twenty-first century education is taking shape, in which businesses play a vital role as vehicles of lifelong learning.

Measurement by success

At Unipart, they believe that it is important 'to enable [employees] to succeed, not to test them for failure.'[92] This means that efforts to develop the individual's creative potential are monitored using positive, rather than negative, outcomes as indicators of performance.

One set of outcomes is based on the quantitative benefits to the firm as a whole. For example, in 1996, Unipart estimated that its culture of learning had resulted in a 30 per cent rise in productivity levels, coupled with a £864 million increase in sales revenues and £32.6 million in profits. In 1998, Unipart announced its seventh consecutive year of record breaking growth with sales exceeding £1.1 billion. While it is difficult to establish precise causal linkages between the company's commercial success and skills development of its employees, the firm does look for evidence that employees are applying what they learn at Unipart U. A primary indicator of skills application is the level of participation in creative problem-solving teams. For example, the company estimates that in its newer companies a minimum of 30 per cent of its employees are involved in an OCC circle, while some of its more established factories are achieving involvement as high as 100 per cent.

A more qualitative means of measuring success is through the process of dissemination. Unipart has instituted multiple pathways for knowledge and progress to be shared with an audience. One pathway, as mentioned previously, is a website that serves as a database for all of the lessons learned through the creative problem solving process. Another pathway is the quarterly recognition ceremonies where OCC teams and individuals are publicly congratulated and their achievements are presented to an audience of peers and senior managers. The 'Mark-in-Action Award', a more individual measure of success, is presented to teams and individuals who have been nominated by peers and managers or customers for demonstrating outstanding customer service. Over 1,700 of these awards have been presented to date. Grapevine, Unipart's video programme, functions as yet another vehicle for recording and disseminating the advancements of company employees. At a more private level, individuals work with Unipart staff to monitor their progress in meeting the goals they have set for themselves in their own personal development plan.

A 'safe place to fail'

The fact that Unipart is careful not to discourage its employees with 'tests for failure' is precisely the reason why its employees are willing to take risks and learn from their mistakes. Take Judith Harris, for example. Judith joined Unipart in 1988 as a personal assistant. In 1996, after eight years and a series of promotions, she is became a Product Marketing Manager for Unipart International and is now leading a special project. So how does Unipart ensure that employees like Judith stay on the learning path and take the risks that accompany creative learning? The answer, according to Judith, is that at Unipart 'there is always someone you can call on, or a course you could take ... and as long as you're up front about things, you are encouraged to try new things. It is okay to make mistakes here.'[93]

Judith, like many of Unipart's employees who have pushed the boundaries of their creative potential, relied on a combination of trusting, supportive relationships and tangible opportunities for developing her skills and self-awareness. For example, she was offered a half day off work each week to work towards a Certificate in Management Studies , as well as the chance to explore other career options by spending time working in different company departments. Like the other creative environments we have explored in this book, Unipart validates the gains that arise from uncertainty and diffuses fears around the costs of failure. It is, Judith explains, 'a safe place to fail'.[94]

Conclusion

Unipart offers several lessons for developing a creative learning environment within an existing organisation. It has deliberately worked to infuse the whole of the firm and its surrounding networks of relationships with opportunities to learn, rather than restricting learning to one part of the firm. It encourages employees to identify problems and to take risks in pursuing new ideas. It recognises that people's performance at work is also integrally linked to their lives beyond, and finds ways to tie family learning, health and broader personal development to the resources it offers for work-based learning. The outcomes it pays attention to range from individual qualification and performance to the quality of working relationships, and it is constantly making the link between smaller scale innovation and overall business success. It recognises that problem solving teams do not need to exist indefinitely, but can be drawn together for a period of time and then reintegrated into the wider organisation. Finally, rather than drawing solely on outside institutions to provide knowledge and skills, it has created the capacity to generate and value them from within.

5

Lessons from case studies

Educating to maximise creative potential is a difficult but essential task. Rather than simply adding to the list of requirements for learners and educators, the examples we have studied have acted as creative exemplars by finding new structures, new ways to generate and share knowledge, and new forms of assessment to gauge its value. They come from different sectors and work with very different groups of learners. They range from the new knowledge industries to old manufacturing firms, from traditional university faculties to the most deprived school-age communities. But they share characteristics that provide important lessons for policy. If governments want to nurture the creative potential of their citizens, education and skills frameworks must be reshaped to accommodate these lessons.

START SMALL AND GROW OUTWARDS

Many of the programmes we have studied started as small scale ventures that took time to grow. Rather than trying to change everything all at once, they began with the seed of an idea and developed it over time. HEAF began as a programme in one school. Waterloo started its co-operative education programme in one department and now involves 50 per cent of its undergraduates. As they have grown in scale, they have also expanded outwards through the different kinds of network. Their reach is measured not only by their level of funding, or the number of participants at a given time, but by their links to wider communities – past students, interested professionals, employers, families and so on. Over time, these networks have become a vital part of the programmes' educational value.

TAKE ENVIRONMENT SERIOUSLY

Alongside a strong focus on individual learners, these programmes pay great attention to the structure and atmosphere of the learning environment. Rather than simply following the structure of existing institutional systems, as most schools and colleges still do, they have reshaped themselves to fit the knowledge and goals that their learners are seeking to achieve. Unipart has deliberately created an atmosphere in which experimentation and interaction are valued beyond existing work roles, and its physical environment reinforces the value of creativity. HEAF has established a safe, stimulating learning environment that encourages its students to forge connections between different aspects of their lives. Citizen Schools has shaped out-of-school learning environments around professional and vocational domains, rather than traditional classroom structures. The programmes also show that most productive learning comes from interaction between learners and the wider environment, and from the experience of shaping one's environment over time.

MATCH HIGH EXPECTATIONS WITH THE SECURITY TO TAKE RISKS

All of the programmes we have studied start with the view that their students are capable of performing well in a range of contexts, and that their ability to perform can be continuously improved. This improvement in effectiveness is one of the primary motivators for developing creative potential. However, they also create bonds of trust and shared understanding that make it possible to redefine failure as a positive and beneficial experience. Unipart makes it explicit that overcoming failure is essential to longer-term success. HEAF begins every learning session with exercises to remind students of their need to trust and support each other. Waterloo encourages students to experiment with work environments that stretch the boundaries of their specalised knowledge. Hyper Island and Citizen Schools both encourage the view that problems are solved through repeated attempts, and that the fastest route to an end point is not always the best long-term solution.

INVOLVE A WIDE FIELD OF SUPPORTERS AND EXPERTS

None of the programmes we have studied draw their knowledge from only one source. They explicitly work to combine different sources of expertise and insight, and ensure that the learner is a primary contributor to the process of knowledge creation. For example, Unipart's OCC circles, Hyper Island's 'live projects' and Citizen Schools' apprenticeships all draw together people with diverse knowledge and experience, and focus them around common goals. They are not seeking to inject knowledge into their students but to enable them to construct it for themselves. This knowledge creation takes place with reference to multiple sources, people and standards of performance, ensuring that the value of what learners do is always related to real-world problems and existing practice.

Another implication of this lesson is that the learning project is constantly building networks outwards into the communities that are relevant to it, whether professional, social or local. Citizen Schools is perhaps the clearest example, creating 'virtual villages' of support for young people learning their way around new domains. Hyper Island has formalised its network building through its mentoring and student databases. HEAF, likewise, creates a network of support and knowledge exchange for its students as they move on to college, and works to draw in its surrounding community.

LOOK FOR PROBLEMS, NOT ANSWERS

Rather than fixing challenges in advance, these projects encourage learners to identify problems for themselves before trying to solve them. Unipart has an established procedure for approving and supporting creative problem solving, which registers goals identified by employees and gives them time to achieve them. Waterloo University encourages students and employers to create specific projects, rather than just fitting students around existing work roles. Hyper Island expects students to identify gaps in their knowledge, in order to complement and enhance the formal course structure. The knowledge gained is also fed back into the way future courses are designed and planned. This process, of identifying and defining problems before they are tackled, is essential to becoming an independent and creative learner. This problem-finding capacity is almost never included in conventional educational frameworks because of the need to cover predefined curricula and meet standardised criteria.

COMBINE DIFFERENT KINDS OF KNOWLEDGE

The projects we have studied all work to integrate different kinds of knowledge into the learning experience. HEAF focuses on relating personal awareness and inter-personal skills to the formation of academic and career goals. Hyper Island combines technical and design courses with project management and business skills. Unipart encourages employees to use the company as a learning resource for all aspects of their lives and to involve wider family and community members as well. Waterloo has structured its academic year around the alternation of academic and hands-on learning. In all of the examples, students are wrapping their understanding of themselves and their learning, and the relationships and techniques which support them, around the specific course content or problem they are addressing. In all of the examples, students draw on a wide range of sources – expert instruction, technical information, peer assessment, user consultation and so on – to develop their skills and abilities.

CONNECT LEARNING TO REAL-WORLD OUTCOMES AND DOMAINS

All of the projects studied relate learning explicitly to concrete, immediate outcomes that make a difference to others. Through applying theory to practice in a Waterloo work placement, learning from a professional apprentice-teacher in Citizen Schools or developing a new media project at Hyper Island, students are constantly relating knowledge and skills to a range of meaningful contexts. They are continuously learning that their knowledge and skills can have a direct, immediate, impact rather than being reserved only for future use.

Students are also learning how to make choices informed by direct experience, a skill that is increasingly valuable as the number of available options continues to grow. This combination of real-time application with longer-term development is a key to employability and successful lifelong learning.

CREATIVITY DOESN'T COME CHEAP

All of the programmes we studied found that they had to invest serious time, effort and resources before they began to reap rewards. As Stephen Denning, Programme Director for Knowledge Management at the World Bank, says, '[knowledge management] doesn't run on air: it does take money'. Work placements at Waterloo University cost more than the average academic course, but the students have acquired a reputation for leadership and creativity that makes them some of the most sought after in the country. HEAF requires extra investment in facilities and courses, but every one of its students so far has gone on to higher education, in comparison with 20 per cent from the surrounding community.

6

Policies for creativity

These lessons might seem easy to absorb. But the structures that govern education systems, the pressure of exams and assessment, and the attitudes of parents, professionals and the media all hold change back. Perhaps the most important barrier is the need to cover existing commitments and curriculum requirements – real change and creativity are hard to achieve when people are overstretched.

The danger of introducing new requirements and expectations in education is that they will simply be grafted onto existing structures – that they will add to the pressure on institutions without actually changing them. To avoid this danger, we must identify the core elements of an education system that enable people to apply their knowledge creatively, and analyse the steps needed to achieve such a system from our starting position.

A TWIN TRACK STRATEGY

A strategy for change rests on the relationship between two key factors: the level of innovation at the edges of the mainstream system and the extent to which the core of the system can adapt and respond. The first depends partly on creating a new, wider infrastructure of learning. This is also essential in providing opportunities to learn and apply knowledge in a wide range of contexts. That is why the new lifelong learning institutions (the University for Industry, out-of-school study centres, firm-based universities, community lifelong learning centres, technology laboratories, and so on) are so important. However, unless these innovators can connect strongly to the core of the system, they will be unable to reach their full potential. This means we must recognise the need to change the central institutions and frameworks which govern education.

CURRICULUM

If we accept the need for change in the core of the system, then we must also recognise the need for curriculum reform. The structure and content of the National Curriculum are more influential in the UK than in almost any other country. It has had many positive effects, not least enabling and reinforcing the 'standards' agenda that currently dominates the UK's approach to education reform. It has helped to create unprecedented consistency, transparency and accountability in the education system. It has also contributed to the recognition that basic standards in key subjects and disciplines, particularly Maths and English, are an essential foundation of any education.

However, if we compare the structure and demands of the National Curriculum against the long-term challenges posed by wider change in society, it becomes clear that they are in danger of becoming a brake on progress, rather than a guarantee of high and consistent standards.

The central danger is that the curriculum will become too heavily defined by content, at the expense of *depth of understanding* and *breadth of application*. The range of subjects covered, the number of topics within each subject and the demands of the assessment regime all push implicitly towards forms of teaching and learning dominated by students' ability to reproduce what they know under the conditions in which they have learned them. In many cases, the need to cover the minimum requirements and meet standard performance targets militates *against* forms of teaching and learning which encourage students to apply knowledge in relevant and unfamiliar settings, and to understand the underlying structure of the disciplines they study. Added to this is the fact that when curriculum subjects are structured, specified and assessed as distinct individual areas, they are more likely to be taught and learned separately, making it more difficult to develop models of inter-disciplinary knowledge and learning.

None of this automatically follows from the specification of compulsory content and subjects, but it is nonetheless a product of the structure, breadth and assessment regime that flow from the curriculum.

To develop the kinds of skills and knowledge increasingly demanded of learners, we must shift from a model of the curriculum based primarily on the formal specification of content, towards a more fluid but no less rigorous definition based on *practice*. We should be able to understand the curriculum as what happens in practice, and base it on direct assessments of the performance of learners in a range of contexts.

What would a curriculum based on the need for creative application of knowledge look like? We would suggest the following characteristics:

- Learning would be structured mainly through **projects**. A project is a piece of work, combining disparate resources, people and types of knowledge, to achieve a goal or concrete outcome. Some projects would be individual, while many would be group-based.

- Problems and goals would not be completely predefined by the curriculum. Students would repeatedly practice **identifying and solving problems**, rather than having them placed before them.
- Learning would take place in a **range of contexts** and use a range of methods. Projects would not all be research-based or within a traditional classroom environment. Students would be involved in *doing* as much as in thinking or knowing.
- Knowledge and learning gains would be **assessed from different perspectives** – including that of the learner. Alongside more traditional, teacher-centred assessment, students' work would be evaluated by field experts, peers, parents and so on. It would be evaluated for different kinds of skills and knowledge – inter-personal, thinking strategies, self-organisation, depth of understanding and so on.
- **Thinking and self-assessment** would be embedded across the curriculum. Students would focus particularly on learning to make connections between different contexts – the transfer and application of knowledge across different domains.
- Skills would be **revisited and practiced over time**, so that knowledge gained earlier in an educational career could be applied creatively to new problems.
- Students would gain **depth of understanding in a number of disciplines**, or domains of knowledge, including traditional academic subjects. They would also learn explicitly how to combine inter-disciplinary knowledge in completing a project goal.

It is vital to recognise that this kind of curriculum would be no less demanding or rigorous than one based on traditional subjects. In fact, students would be called upon to do more with the knowledge they have gained, and to present evidence of their understanding. In particular, the shift towards a project-based model of learning increases the need for rigorous understanding of subjects like mathematics, language, science or literature, as knowledge must be applied toward the production of tangible outcomes.

Skills specifications

Alongside the content and structure of learning, students would develop their skills and competencies across the range of learning activities, within a clear and detailed specification of the clusters of skills identified in chapter three:

- self-organisation, including forming and articulating goals
- personal and inter-personal

- information management
- risk management
- disciplinary and inter-disciplinary knowledge in a given number of domains
- reflection and evaluation.

These specifications could be developed from the existing Key Skills specifications, but with an important proviso. Rather than developing separate certificates or qualifications, they would be embedded in the structure of every subject discipline and evaluated through context-specific, performance-based assessment. This assessment would be according to common standards but would be undertaken by a range of assessors, rather than a single examiner or teacher. The levels of skill achieved would be recorded in a learning portfolio, as part of a record of continuous personal development.

A coherent structure

To make such a curriculum work, we need a basic structure that makes it practically achievable. We are arguing for more diverse and fluid forms of learning, with a wider range of assessment and more complex patterns of scheduling and provision. Without a robust, replicable structure around which these diverse learning activities can be organised, such an approach would not work. Can we find a model to organise learning which is practically achievable, replicable and rigorous, and feasible for teachers and schools?

We would argue that the components of such a structure are already beginning to emerge at the edges of the school and lifelong learning systems. However, without further development there is a danger that they will continue to hover at the margins and fail to reach their full potential.

There are three central components.

Project

The basic organisational unit, or module, around which learning and skills development are planned. Through the design, completion and review of a project, students gain knowledge, skills and understanding. Knowledge content is structured in ways that reflect the context in which it is applied, rather than organised around conventional school subjects. Alongside the various learning gains that a project can achieve, it has a concrete product or outcome beyond its educational value.

Portfolio

The learning portfolio is the central spine of the new educational career, but it is yet to be fully recognised as such. The portfolio is a record of progress and outcomes, combining evidence of achievement, assessment from different experts, goals and objectives formed by the learner, and self-evaluation. It is the central instrument for organising and recording the progress of a learner over time. As information technology develops, a growing range of integrated portfolio models combine the elements of a learner's progress on CD-rom or online.

Portfolio management is vital to lifelong learning and creativity, and to employability in the new economy. It is a way for learners to revisit and build on earlier learning gains, and to integrate and co-ordinate evidence and evaluation from a wide range of sources.

Portfolio development is also a group process: at Hyper Island, dedicated time is given to production teams to discuss, develop and modify their portfolios as a group. For school-age students, the portfolio would be a tool for recording and assessing learning progress in a number of fields, and a form of evidence to present to employers, colleges and universities. It would include formal course credits, direct evidence of applied skills and personal development, assessments from out-of-school placements and completed project work.

The UK has two seeds of a new learning portfolio – the Progress File, piloted as a replacement for the National Record of Achievement, and the new lifelong learning log being developed by the University for Industry. The Progress File, which has been piloted in some UK schools, is an early model. However, it is not fully developed and has not occupied a central place in the assessment framework because of the continuing dominance of examinations. The lifelong learning log has been recognised as central to the effectiveness of University for Industry initiatives but has yet to be used widely in practice.

Broker
The final part of the jigsaw is the creation of a role to weave together the different projects, placements and resources needed for students to pursue a balanced project-based curriculum.

School–community brokers would be responsible for managing the interface between academic and real world learning. Their role would be to cultivate and maintain a network of parents, community members, professionals and organisations on which students and teachers can draw for learning opportunities and creative input. They would be responsible for maintaining a database of placement opportunities, resources and contacts. They would also advise students on developing and planning their portfolios, and liaise with subject-specialist teachers on the learning and assessment strategies for individual students and project teams.

At the moment, in most schools there is no dedicated professional responsible for managing the interface between the school as an institution and its surrounding community. The school–community broker would do exactly that. This brokerage role is beginning to emerge through the provision of out-of-school learning and in areas such as Business Education Links. Again, however, it has yet to have an impact on the provision of mainstream school education.

The combination of these three elements makes a curriculum for creativity a practical possibility, rather than a wish list. Figure 2 sets out the relationship between them, the ways in which different elements connect students to the wider learning environment

Getting there

Achieving this kind of change in an education system already straining to adapt to reform is no easy task. It requires radical, long-term action from policymakers, practitioners, firms, universities and the wider community.

The National Curriculum for England and Wales has just been through its first ten-year review. The changes proposed increased flexibility in some areas and added new content in others. However, they left the basic structure more

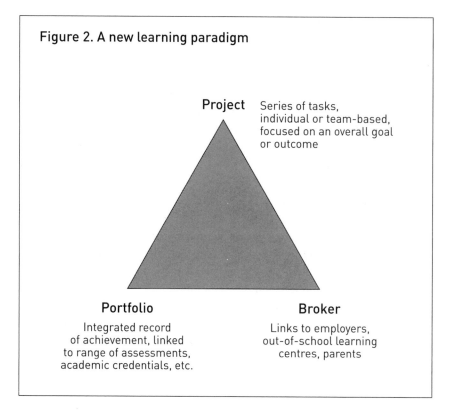

Figure 2. A new learning paradigm

Project — Series of tasks, individual or team-based, focused on an overall goal or outcome

Portfolio — Integrated record of achievement, linked to range of assessments, academic credentials, etc.

Broker — Links to employers, out-of-school learning centres, parents or less intact. This means that the assessment and teaching methods needed are also relatively unchanged. One of the most important innovations to emerge from the review process has been the recognition that a rolling programme of development and reform, rather than a monolithic review of everything once a decade, is necessary for continued progress. New approaches to curriculum development – through the introduction of citizenship, for example, and the integration of teacher training, information technology support and revised curriculum requirements in primary literacy and numeracy – are beginning to point the way to a new approach.

This new, evolutionary approach to curriculum reform, which integrates formal requirements with innovation and development in *practice*, must be sustained and strengthened. But to succeed, it must be sustained by ambitious objectives.

These objectives must be informed by the recognition that depth of understanding and breath of application cannot be developed properly without creating time and space for them. The demands of curriculum coverage, particularly in the number of topics covered within each subject, constrain the ability of teachers and students to develop the skills and abilities that we now know we need. This means that government, as part of a rolling programme of reform, needs to make a bold and difficult choice about the level of content required by the school curriculum.

Within ten years we should have achieved the following goals:

- reducing curriculum content and time by half, to create space for depth of disciplinary understanding and for breadth of application
- introducing a system of IT-based learning portfolios for every school student, to give a strong link to the new lifelong learning infrastructure
- developing detailed specifications and assessment standards for the six new clusters of skills, and making them integral to every area of education between birth and nineteen
- appointing a minimum of two school–community brokers to every school
- creating an out-of-school learning infrastructure that provides opportunities for project-based and placement learning for every school student
- every secondary school pupil should complete at least two extended projects a year, as part of the overall curriculum
- a new model of work experience, moving from the current two-week placement to more extended placements and project work
- half of undergraduate degrees should include at least one extended work placement.

The reduction of curriculum content would not take place all in one go. Instead, requirements would be gradually reduced while the demands of depth, breadth of application, and new forms of assessment were gradually built up. We are not arguing that the curriculum should become any less challenging to learn or to deliver, but that a new set of priorities should complement and gradually supersede the structures that currently dominate. Rigour and understanding in traditional subjects would remain a foundation of educational achievement. But the *ways* in which this knowledge is used would also become one of the primary criterion of educational performance.

Cross-disciplinary teaching and learning

Restructuring the curriculum in this way relies on the development of new, rigorous forms of cross-disciplinary teaching and learning. This should be a priority for curriculum and development in schools and for teacher training.

There are a range of ways to integrate different components of the National Curriculum, for example through the use of unifying themes or concepts that draw on content from each discipline. Teachers should be encouraged to work together in teams to develop inter-disciplinary curricula that incorporate national content requirements, and schools should be encouraged to experiment with different timetables for integrating subject-based and inter-disciplinary approaches. Some may decide to allocate a particular portion of the school day towards inter-disciplinary teaching, while others may experiment with ways of interspersing more extended periods of inter-disciplinary teaching into the traditional subject-based curriculum.

Teacher training and professional development should include a stronger focus on forms of multi-disciplinary teaching and learning. They should have a basic understanding of the principles underlying each of the major disciplines and the opportunity to practice developing and delivering curriculum that crosses disciplinary boundaries.

EXTENDING OUTWARDS

If these are the goals for the core school curriculum, they will not work without major change to the wider infrastructure of learning. One of the central lessons of our case studies is that the skills we need are developed through interaction and collaboration between different sectors, and by applying knowledge in a range of contexts. In order to do this, we must accelerate the creation of a learning infrastructure that extends far beyond formal education into firms, museums, libraries, community institutions and public spaces.

Some steps are already being taken in this direction. The New Opportunities Fund is creating out-of-school study centres in half of secondary schools and a third of primary schools over the next three years. The University for Industry is creating new relationships between education and employers. The National Grid for Learning will have the potential to link many different institutions in creating and sharing knowledge. However, more ambitious policies are needed to bolster the structural reform of the curriculum and provide lifelong learning opportunities to more people. To achieve this, Government should:

- use the new Lifelong Learning Partnerships to encourage collaboration across sectors in funding and organising learning
- expand the Study Support programme to create more out-of-school hours study centres, and hands-on learning opportunities; these centres should be located as far as possible out of schools and in other community institutions
- create a series of local and national databases, linked to the National Grid for Learning, that provide access to: learning opportunities (organisations that can provide placements or courses), skill sharers (people with knowledge or skills that they are willing to share in and out-of-school contexts) and dissemination websites (presenting, debating and sharing knowledge about innovation in a series of individual and inter-disciplinary subject areas)
- develop financial incentives to encourage collaboration and skills investment across sectors, rather than just within them.

INVESTING IN KNOWLEDGE

The hard economic problem surrounding skills investment remains who is going to pay for it. Real government spending on education and training has risen steadily for several decades, but demand increasingly outstrips the capacity of general tax revenues to pay for it. Most of the education infrastructure has expanded and improved its productivity in conventional terms – for example, UK universities have increased their student numbers massively while driving down costs per head. But this kind of change is finite – the existing institutions and methods will not be able to continue forever without more radical change. In any case, the examples in this report show that different kinds of skills need different kinds of learning environment.

This is one reason why the new instruments for lifelong learning are being developed – the Individual Learning Account, for example. But more is needed if investment is going to be shared right across society, rather than only in the high-skill, high value-added realms of the economy where knowledge already brings high rewards.

Government should therefore create a tax credit for employers who provide structured work placements in partnership with secondary schools, universities and further education colleges, following the Canadian example. In the longer term, the corporate tax regime should reflect firms' investment in skills and knowledge in a wide range of ways, including the extent to which their facilities are open to members of the wider community and the degree to which firms release employees to serve as resources for educational programmes.

The idea of a skills or training levy has provoked controversy in the UK, with employers arguing that they are already faced with enough tax and regulatory burdens, and that a general levy is an unproductive form of investment in the specific skills they need. One refinement of the idea, already in operation in Singapore, is to create a levy specifically tied to grants for employee training. The Skills Development Fund levies 1 per cent of wages for employees earning less than $1,000 per month, and reinvests it in training programmes to which companies can apply. The fund has contributed to a general increase in skills investment in Singapore since its introduction in 1979.

Policies that help to offset the risk that employees will move on before investment training brings a return are also needed. Offering graduated rewards, such as stock options to returning employees, is one way to do this. However, we should also recognise the importance of other kinds of value to increasing employee loyalty and commitment – the social value of trust, the community value of opening learning facilities to family and community members, the psychological value of being respected and being able to contribute, the confidence inspired by the knowledge that what you are doing at a given time is helping to increase your potential for the future.

Rather than looking at skills investment as a zero-sum financial game, government should be seeking to maximise value through shared investment. This means more than just spreading the burden of training costs: it means encouraging the development of learners who can apply their skills independently and who therefore increase the value of educational investment by being able to spread its gains across a wider range of contexts. In policy terms this means further work to develop models and measures of learning gains across organisations and in people's personal lives, rather than simply in relation to their own career and income prospects.

SKILLS SPECIFICATIONS

The Key Skills qualification is in danger of taking a wrong turn. The danger is that a certificate will emerge that relies too much on standardised, decontextualised forms of assessment. Evidence from employers suggests that conventional certificates in 'soft' skills such as communication are largely irrelevant to their needs.

Instead, we should work towards a clearer and more detailed framework of skills clusters, based on performance-based assessment and judged in relation to context, rather than relying on standardised testing or on task-based competence assessment, as with the current vocational framework, which does not take enough account of the need to perform tasks in a range of contexts.

These specifications should not be restricted to schools and colleges but should be developed in conjunction with employers and institutions with specialist expertise in particular fields. The specifications could form part of an extended Investors in People standard, as well as part of the base of a learning portfolio.

REWARDING CREATIVITY IMAGINATIVELY

Finally, we need ways to develop and reward creativity in the way that education is delivered and skills applied. Measures to stimulate this could include:

- rewarding teachers, educators and policymakers for creativity and innovation; a professional contract that rewarded creative contribution rather than hours worked or minimum standards met could have powerful, far-reaching effects
- Skills Olympics, where students gather to demonstrate problem solving and creative abilities in meeting community or skills challenges, rewarded with seed funding and expert support to develop creative ideas further.

CONCLUSION

People need skills that will enable them to thrive across a diverse, fast-changing and demanding range of situations. The economy needs people who are able to draw on their full potential to contribute ideas and know-how to the work they do. Yet they cannot develop this ability just by trying to get more and more conventional qualifications – the qualifications will become less useful in practice and the education system will become overloaded by the pressure to produce a growing set of outcomes. The challenge is to support and finance forms of learning which add immediate value to the contexts in which learning is taking place, and at the same time contribute to the longer-term abilities and prospects of the learner.

This report has shown that it is possible to educate for creativity within any sector of society. The education system cannot produce the creative learners that we increasingly need without being relieved of some of the other pressures it faces. One way to relieve this pressure is to involve other sectors in delivering and assessing learning. As we gradually build a broader infrastructure, the opportunities for learning will continue to expand. However, unless the core of the curriculum also changes, we will fail to make the most of these new opportunities. The core curriculum can cover a wide range of subject areas and topics, but risks teaching in ways that do not lead to depth of understanding or the ability to apply knowledge widely. If we want these qualities, we must recognise the need to focus on a smaller number of disciplines and topics, and help to ensure that sudents learn to apply what they know creatively, both in school and beyond. We have argued that this is the best long-term option. Though difficult to achieve, it is essential to ensuring a creative and competitive future.

Notes

1. Leadbeater C, 1998, 'Welcome to the Knowledge Economy' in Hargreaves I and Christie I, eds, *Tomorrow's Politics*, Demos, London

2. See Coyle D , 1997, *The Weightless World: Thriving in the Digital Age*, Capstone Ltd, Oxford.

3. Godbout TM, 'Employment change and sectoral distribution in 10 countries, 1970-90', *Monthly Labor Review Online*, vol 116, no 10, October 1993, Bureau of Labor Statistics http://stats.bls.gov/opub/mlt/1993/10/art1full.pdf.

4. Ibid.

5. Skills & Enterprise Network, 1999, 'Europe's Labour Market', *Skills and Enterprise Briefing*, issue 2/99, [Author], London.

6. These include: advertising, architecture, arts and antiques, crafts, design, designer fashion, film, leisure software, music, performing arts, publishing, software and computer services, television and radio.

7. NACCCE, 'The Challenge for Education' , in *All Our Futures: Creativity, Culture and Education*, DFEE, London, p19.

8. DCMS, 1998, Creative Industries Mapping Document.

9. Herzenberg S, Alic JA and Wial H, 1998, *New Rules for a New Economy: Employment and Opportunity in Postindustrial America*, Cornell University Press, New York.

10. *Skills and Enterprise Network Briefing*, issue 2/99.

11. Robinson P, 1997, 'Labour Market Studies- United Kingdom', European Commission, quoted in J Philpott, 1999 'Behind the Buzzword: 'Employability', *Economic Report*, vol 12, no 10, January/February, Employment Policy Institute.

12. Barley SR, 1996, *The New World of Work*, British-North American Committee, London.

13. Zuboff S, 1989, *In the Age of the Smart Machine*, Basic Books, New York, quoted in Barley, *The New World of Work*.

14. Skills & Enterprise Network, 1999 'Challenging Future for Many Graduates', *Skills and Enterprise EXECUTIVE*, issue 2/99, [Author], London.

15. Kanter RM, 1995, *World Class: Thriving Locally in the Global Economy*, Simon & Schuster, New York, p151.

16. See Handy C, 1989, *The Age of Unreason*, Arrow Books, London; Robertson J, 1985, *Future Work*, Gower Publishing Company Ltd, Aldershot; Bridges W, 1995, *Jobshift*, NB Books, London; Arthur MB, 1994, 'The boundaryless career: a new perspective for organizational inquiry', *Journal of Organizational Behaviour*, 15, pp295-306.

17. Guile, D and Fonda N, 1999, *Managing Learning for Added Value*, Institute of Personnel and Development, London, p39.

18. Arulampalam W and Booth AL, 1998, 'Labour Market Flexibility and Skills Acquisition: Is there a trade-off?' in Atkinson AB and Hills J, *Exclusion, Employment and Opportunity*, Centre for the Analysis of Social Exclusion, London, p66.

19. Green FG et al, 1998, 'Are British Workers Getting More Skilled?' in Atkinson

and Hills, *Exclusion, Employment and Opportunity*; See also Carlton S and Soulsby J, 1999, *Learning to Grow Older and Bolder: A policy discussion on learning later in life*, Leicester, NIACE.

20. Murnane RJ and Levy F, 1996, *Teaching the New Basic Skills: Principles for educating children to thrive in a changing economy*, The Free Press, New York.

21. Skills and Enterprise Network, 'Skill Needs in Britain', *Skills and Enterprise Briefing*, Issue 3/99.

22. Ibid.

23. Ibid.

24. Jobs for the Future, 'Business Participation in Welfare-to-Work: Lessons from the United States', paper given at the Business Forum conference, *Welfare-to-Work: Lessons from America*, 20-21 January 1999, New York.

25. Crouch C, Finegold D and Sako M, 1999, *Are Skills the Answer?*, Oxford University Press, Oxford, p21.

26. Ibid.

27. Atkinson and Hills, *Exclusion, Employment and Opportunity*.

28. Davis S and Botkin J, 1994, *The Monster Under the Bed*, Simon & Schuster, New York, quoted in Tapscott D, 1998, *Growing Up Digital: The rise of the next generation*, McGraw-Hill, NewYork, p152.

29. London Skills Forecasting Unit, 1998, *Annual Report*, [Author], London; Institute of Personal Development, 1999, 'The IPD Survey Report 2: Recruitment', [Author], London; Barley, *The New World of Work.*; IFF Research Ltd, 1998, 'Skills Needs in Great Britain and Ireland', [Author], London.

30. Kanter, *World Class*, p155.

31. Murnane and Levy, *Teaching the New Basic Skills*.

32. Ibid.

33. Ibid.

34. Wah L, 'Making Knowledge Stick', *Management Review*, May 1999.

35. Gardner H, 1993, *Multiple Intelligences: The theory in practice*, Basic Books, New York; Perkins D, 1995, *Outsmarting IQ: The emerging science of learnable intelligence*, Free Press, New York.

36. Wah, 'Making Knowledge Stick'.

37. Perkins, *Outsmarting IQ*, p269.

38. See Bereiter Cl and Scardamalia M, 1993, *Surpassing Ourselves: An inquiry into the nature and implications of expertise*, Open Court, Chicago.

39. Perkins, *Outsmarting IQ,*, p256.

40. Csikszentmihalyi M, 1996, *Creativity: Flow and the psychology of discovery and invention*, HarperCollins, New York, p95.

41. Ibid, p95-96.

42. Dweck CS and Bempechat J, 1980, 'Children's Theories of Intelligence: Consequences for learning', in Paris SG, Olson GM and Stevenson HW, eds, *Learning and Motivation in the Classroom*, Erlbaum, Hillsdale, New Jersey, quoted in Perkins, *Outsmarting IQ*, p277.

43. Perkins, *Outsmarting IQ*, p275.

44. Csiksentmihalyi, *Creativity*, p127.

45. Ferguson R and Clay P with Snipes JC and Roaf P, 1996, *Youthbuild in Developmental Perspective: A formative evaluation of the Youthbuild Demonstration Project*, Department of Urban Studies and Planning, MIT, Cambridge, Massachusetts, p134.

46. Ibid.

47. Ferguson et al, *Youthbuild in Developmental Perspective*; Perkins, *Outsmarting IQ,*, ; Csiksentmihalyi M, 1997, *Living Well: The psychology of Everyday Life*, Weidenfeld and Nicolson, London.

48. Csiksentmihalyi, *Living Well*, p126.

49. Perkins, *Outsmarting IQ*.

50. Csiksentmihalyi, *Creativity*, p28.

51. Perkins, *Outsmarting IQ*.

52. See Darmon I, Hadjivassiliou K, Sommerlad E, Stern E, Turbin J with Danau D, 1998, 'Continuing vocational training: key issues', in Coffield F, ed, 1998, *Learning at Work*, Policy Press, Bristol; Oates T, 1999, [unpublished document] 'Analysing and describing competence- critical perspectives'; Oates T and Fettes P, 1998, *Key Skills*

Strategy Paper, Qualifications and Curriculum Authority, London; Ferguson et al, *Youthbuild in Developmental Perspective*.

53. Perkins, *Outsmarting IQ*, p227.

54. See Bentley T, 1998, *Learning Beyond the Classroom: Education for a changing world*, Routledge, London; also Wolfe A, 1998, 'Fifteen Years of core and key skills: some cautionary tales', a background paper for the Employability and Key Skills Sub-group, Skills Task Force, London; Wolfe A, 'Rotten core could kill', *The Times Educational Supplement*, 14 August 1998.

55. Ferguson et al, *Youthbuild in Developmental Perspective*.

56. Erikson EH, 1963, *Childhood and Society*, WW Norton & Co, New York, p252.

57. Ibid, p254.

58. Mulgan G and Wilkinson H, 1995, 'Well-being and Time', *The Time Squeeze*, Demos Quarterly issue 5, Demos, London, p6.

59. Csiksentmihalyi M and Csiksentmihalyi IS, eds, 1988, *Optimal Experience: Psychological studies of flow in consciousness*, Cambridge University Press, Cambridge, p32.

60. Reinhard B, 'In Devising After-school Programs, Commitment is Key', *Education Week*, vol XVII, no 30, 8 April 1998.

61. Gardner M, 'Children Take to Being a Professional', *Christian Science Monitor*, 21 August 1996.

62. Citizen Schools, [unpublished document], 'Citizen Schools: An Adventure in Learning', Boston, Massachusetts.

63. 'Off the Cuff: Q & A with Irvel Syvestre, Citizens Schools student', *Boston Sunday Globe*, 30 August 1998.

64. Ibid.

65. Ibid.

66. Ibid.

67. Harlem Educational Activities Fund, '1997-1998: Annual Report', p24.

68. Ibid, p18.

69. Harlem Educational Activities Fund, [unpublished document], 'High Expectations Spring-Into-High School Curriculum', p3.

70. Ibid, p4.

71. Harlem Educational Activities Fund, '1997-1998: Annual Report', p29.

72. Hyper Island, [Unpublished Document], 'Hyper Island School of New Media Design', p9.

73. Ibid.

74. Ibid.

75. This site is not open to people outside of the Hyper Island network.

76. University of Waterloo was also ranked the 'best overall' university in Canada according to Maclean's magazine national reputational ranking for all Canadian universities from 1992-1998.

77. University of Waterloo, UW Recruiter, www.w.adm.uwaterloo.ca/infocecs/blue_recruiter/blue_frames.html.

78. Ibid.

79. Ibid.

80. Ibid.

81. Companies such as Nortel Networks have hosted up to 75 co-op students at one time and hired over 250 programme graduates.

82. Co-op students in the technical disciplines must complete a minimum of five work terms in order to graduate, and arts students are required to complete at least four

83. University of Waterloo, UW Recruiter, www.w.adm.uwaterloo.ca/infocecs/blue_recruiter/blue_frames.html.

84. Duncan A, [unpublished paper], 'Unipart Group of Companies: Uniting stakeholders to build a world class enterprise', prepared at London Business School, p4.

85. Unipart has a agreement with Templeton College library so that staff may have access to all of their books.

86. Unipart has an extensive software library that includes a whole range of personal interest software that staff members can check out and try at home with their families.

87. Eraut M, 1999, 'Learning in the Workplace', presentation given at the ESRC Conference, 'The Learning Society', 6-7 July 1999, Westminster.

88. Duncan A, 'Unipart Group of Companies: Uniting stakeholders to build a world class enterprise'.

89. Bentley, *Learning Beyond the Classroom*.

90. Interview with Ian Campbell, 14 July 1999.

91. Ibid.

92. Conversation with Frank Nigriello and Ian Campbell, 14 July 1999.

93. Duncan A, 'Unipart Group of Companies: Uniting stakeholders to build a world-class enterprise', p11.

94. Ibid.